Football and Risk

This is the first book to look closely at the concept of 'risk' in elite and professional football from a social scientific perspective. Drawing on the wider sociological, criminological and management literature on risk, it shows how football helps us to understand global risk more generally in present-day society.

The book explores how attitudes to risk have shaped the modern football business, and identifies those risks that pose a threat to the sustainability of football in the future. It draws upon the work of theorists including Ulrich Beck, Anthony Giddens and Michel Foucault, as well as digital media sources and policy documents, and covers a range of topics, cases and themes including political, environmental and terrorism risks, technologies, the governance of fans and risk resistance. In the context of the social, globalized and commercialized realm of football, as well as a global pandemic that has had a profound influence on attitudes to risk, the book argues that modern societies' preoccupation with risk has transformed the ways in which modern football is played on the pitch, organized off the pitch, covered in the media and attended by fans.

Including an extended case study of the 2026 World Cup, to be held in the USA, Mexico and Canada, this is a thought-provoking read for any student, researcher or policy-maker with an interest in football, sport, events, sociology, criminology or risk management.

Jan Andre Lee Ludvigsen is Senior Lecturer in International Relations and Politics with Sociology at Liverpool John Moores University, UK. Broadly, Jan's main research areas are within the social and political study of sport, and his research on sport mega-events, security, risk and fandom has been published in journals such as the *International Review for the Sociology of Sport, Journal of Consumer Culture, Leisure Studies* and *Journal of Sport and Social Issues*. He has also authored *Sport Mega-Events, Security and Covid-19: Securing the Football World* (Routledge, 2022).

Critical Research in Football

Series Editors:
Pete Millward, Liverpool John Moores University, UK
Jamie Cleland, University of Southern Australia
Dan Parnell, University of Liverpool, UK
Stacey Pope, Durham University, UK
Paul Widdop, Manchester Metropolitan University, UK

The *Critical Research in Football* book series was launched in 2017 to showcase the inter- and multi-disciplinary breadth of debate relating to 'football'. The series defines 'football' as broader than association football, with research on rugby, Gaelic and gridiron codes also featured. Including monographs, edited collections, short books and textbooks, books in the series are written and/or edited by leading experts in the field whilst consciously also affording space to emerging voices in the area, and are designed to appeal to students, postgraduate students and scholars who are interested in the range of disciplines in which critical research in football connects. The series is published in association with the *Football Collective*, @FB_Collective.
    Available in this series:

Sport Mega-Events, Security and COVID-19
Securing the Football World
Jan Andre Lee Ludvigsen

Integrated Marketing Communications in Football
Argyro Elisavet Manoli

Football and Risk
Trends and Perspectives
Jan Andre Lee Ludvigsen

https://www.routledge.com/Critical-Research-in-Football/book-series/CFSFC

Football and Risk
Trends and Perspectives

Jan Andre Lee Ludvigsen

Routledge
Taylor & Francis Group

LONDON AND NEW YORK

First published 2023
by Routledge
4 Park Square, Milton Park, Abingdon, Oxon OX14 4RN

and by Routledge
605 Third Avenue, New York, NY 10158

Routledge is an imprint of the Taylor & Francis Group, an informa business

© 2023 Jan Andre Lee Ludvigsen

British Library Cataloguing-in-Publication Data
A catalogue record for this book is available from the British Library

Library of Congress Cataloging-in-Publication Data
Names: Ludvigsen, Jan Andre Lee, author.
Title: Football and risk : trends and perspectives / Jan Andre Lee
Ludvigsen.
Description: Abingdon, Oxon ; New York, NY : Routledge, 2022. |
Series: Critical research in football | Includes bibliographical
references and index. |
Identifiers: LCCN 2022012902 | ISBN 9781032301129 (hardback) |
ISBN 9781032301136 (paperback) | ISBN 9781003303480 (ebook)
Subjects: LCSH: Soccer—Social aspects. | Risk—Sociological
aspects. | Risk—Sociological aspects—Case studies. | Sports—
Environmental aspects. | Globalization and sport. | World Cup
(Soccer)—Case studies.
Classification: LCC GV943.9.S64 L84 2022 | DDC 796.334—dc23/
eng/20220525
LC record available at https://lccn.loc.gov/2022012902

ISBN: 978-1-032-30112-9 (hbk)
ISBN: 978-1-032-30113-6 (pbk)
ISBN: 978-1-003-30348-0 (ebk)

DOI: 10.4324/9781003303480

Typeset in Times New Roman
by codeMantra

I dedicate this book to my strong, funny and kind grandfather. My *halabogi*. I will always cherish our memories and smile when thinking about them. To borrow what was one of his favourite phrases when describing anything great, good or positive: you were *'number one'*.

Contents

Acknowledgements

Not uncommonly, a book's acknowledgements page composes a somewhat reflective space to reminisce about, or elaborate on, where the idea for the relevant book initially grew from. To be perfectly honest, I cannot remember an exact moment where the idea underlying this book came into my mind. Rather, I choose to believe that the idea, in a far more time diffuse fashion, was gradually conceived over a manifold of conversations with good colleagues and friends through which my academic interest in risk and football intensified. This book, like all my academic work, has benefited immensely from the support and encouragement I have received over the years. However, the usual disclaimer still applies: any potential errors are entirely my own.

A giant thanks to Simon Whitmore and Rebecca Connor at Routledge for supporting and believing in this book and for their fantastic help and advice. I also extend a huge thanks to Jamie Cleland, the Series Editor of *Critical Research in Football*, for his guidance and constant encouragement when I first proposed this book. Much gratitude is also due to Dan Parnell, Chris Allen, John Hayton, Joe Moran, Dan Feather, Matt Hill, Elizabeth Peatfield and David Tyrer whom I can always go to for useful advice, as well as all my other colleagues in Liverpool John Moores University's departments of International Relations & Politics and Sociology. On other projects, I have been fortunate enough to work or collaborate with scholars who have taught me a whole lot. Therefore, special thanks are also due to Paul Widdop, David Webber, Renan Petersen-Wagner, Mark Turner, Joel Rookwood, Christie Scanlon, Seamus Byrne, Nicholas Wise and others whom I have had the pleasure of working or bouncing off ideas with over the last years. A huge thanks to Jodie Hodgson for advice and help, and to Peter

Millward for his outstanding support, wisdom, friendship and for countless of conversations.

I would like to acknowledge, with the utmost gratitude, my mum, dad, brother, uncle and grandmother who are always there with unconditional support, encouragement, patience and love.

1 Introduction

Kick-off: football and risk

This book is pioneering in its attempt to bring together the two socially important topics of *football* and *risk*, whose relationship and inter-connections are yet to be fully explored in the academic literature. In that sense, it offers a contemporary update of and a novel context for considering sociological risk theories. Risk is not a new concept. Neither is it a recent addition to our vocabularies. However, the employment of the term has mushroomed in political, academic, public and everyday discourses and settings since the early 1990s (Giulianotti, 2009). Perhaps particularly so, following the publication of the German sociologist Ulrich Beck's (1992) landmark text titled *Risk Society: Towards a New Modernity*. From Beck's perspective, risk societies are, on a foundational level, modern societies that are increasingly organized around the responses to and aversion of risks. In line with a progressive and increasingly globalized modern world, the enhanced emphasis on the management and anticipation of potentially catastrophic local, national and transnational risks has had an enormous impact on societies, politics and individual citizens. This powerful backdrop, I capture and update in the social worlds of football.

The risk society is characterized by a heightened reflexivity of individuals towards modernization's potentially disastrous and damaging effects (Giulianotti, 2009). Fundamentally, this is partly due to the notion that '[f]rom natural disasters and terrorism to health and finance, *risk is now everywhere*' (Aradau et al., 2008: 147, emphasis added). As encapsulated most recently and powerfully by the Covid-19 pandemic (Tooze, 2020), the risks of the modern world may be global, potentially catastrophic, inherently unpredictable and uncontrollable. Whilst this will be unpacked in greater depth in Chapter 2, this provides a key

DOI: 10.4324/9781003303480-1

rationale for now revisiting the 'risk society' (Beck, 1992) and for this book overall, which holds tight to the notion that contemporary elite football has not been immune from the marked consequences of the risk society, just as football *has not* been exempt from globalization processes (see e.g., Cleland, 2015; Giulianotti and Robertson, 2009; Millward, 2011), especially given the dynamic inter-connections between risks and globalization (Chapter 2).

As discussed below, there are a few existing studies that use the existing sociological risk frameworks and apply them to football (or sporting) contexts (e.g., Cleland, 2019; Giulianotti and Robertson, 2009; Lee Ludvigsen, 2020, 2021; Toohey, 2008). Moreover, there is a far more substantial bank of research that explores the diverse effects of globalization on football (Chapter 2). The latter repository of literature remains especially relevant here because, following Beck (1992, 1999), the (world) risk society has advanced in parallel with intensifying globalization processes. But even still, there is minimal academic research on the exact risk typologies in football, or the (in)direct implications of the risk society and our preoccupation with risk aversion upon modern-day elite football which is regularly dubbed to be the 'global game'. Significantly, and compared to other mainstream topics or concepts such as identity, gender, globalization or fandom, the sociology of sport 'has yet to witness the emergence of a network of scholars whose defining focus is risk analysis' (Giulianotti, 2009: 541).

Against this backdrop, this book first aims to showcase and elucidate an argument that football, in fact, remains a fruitful, insightful and important site for the social sciences' understandings of risk. Second, it aims to (re-)energize and provide directions for the field of risk analysis in football. The prominence of 'risk' in modern societies (see Beck, 1992, 1999; Giddens, 1990; Lupton, 1999), I argue, has tremendously impacted the ways in which football is organized, managed, policed, attended and represented in the media. As argued, football reflects and accentuates global risk politics, awareness and management, whereas the consequences of the risk society are felt by the popular sport's athletes, fans, the media and commentators, football's governing bodies and those countries or authorities seeking to stage prestigious football championships like the World Cup or European Championship. As I contend, this argument remains important because all this – as situated in football – can shed a light on how societies more broadly are organized and respond to risks that occur across 'exceptional' and 'everyday' contexts.

It is for this reason that, while this book focuses specifically on the importance of *football* to better and critically understand risk, risk cultures and its management, the arguments, implications and case studies of this book can speak to wider mainstream and current debates in the social sciences. As Giulianotti (2009: 553) maintained, sociologists of sport have the opportunity to fill sizable lacunas in the study of risk 'through sport-centered research, and become fully engaged in mainstream social scientific debates by transferring those findings back into the wider field of risk analysis'. Principally, this book is strongly rooted in such a perspective. Whereas it makes a direct scholarly contribution to the sociologies of football and sport with its analysis and future directions, it simultaneously taps into even larger debates at stake within sociology and in the growing critical criminology of sport (Millward et al., in press). In doing so, the book extends a palette of risk theories into football: a domain where they rarely have been applied previously. So, the book seeks to say something about how risks shape individuals, societies, cultures and the social and political orders in the twenty-first century. In that sense, my book consciously responds and attends to Giulianotti's (2009: 541, emphasis added) 'concise *invitation* to sociologists of sport *to enter the field of risk analysis*'. It does so, by throwing a much-needed light on the complex relationship between *global risks* and the *global game*.

Notes on the modern meanings of risk

One rudimentary question that surfaces at this point is what 'risk' *means* exactly. Whilst it is not my intention here to redefine this term, it is, at the same time, both practical and necessary to engage with some of the meanings and sociological definitions or comprehensions of 'risk' that co-exist. Risk is not a static phenomenon (Toohey, 2008) and it is a term that Mythen (2004: 54) describes as 'notoriously slippery'. Increasingly, risk is also a 'notion [that] has become ubiquitous' (Weimer, 2017: 10). Hence, there are no universal definitions available of the term risk that can be generally applied.

However, over the past centuries, the term's meanings have changed significantly and been used in 'far more common and applied to a plethora of situations' (Lupton, 1999: 5).[1] Fundamentally, the transformations in the deployment of the term risk have been hugely influenced by modernization processes. One contemporary way of understanding risk therefore relates to modernity's 'new way of viewing the world and its chaotic manifestations, its contingencies and uncertainties' (ibid.: 6). Indeed, modern risk definitions often centre around the 'future', 'probabilities', 'uncertainties' or even 'dangers'. This naturally relates to Lupton's (1999: 8, emphasis added) observation that: 'Risk is now generally used to relate only to *negative or undesirable* outcomes, not positive outcomes'. And, moreover, the commonly shared idea of risk is associated with 'undesired events in an uncertain future' (Zinn, 2009: 6). Toohey (2008: 430) echoes this and underlines that throughout the 'twentieth century the notion of risk took on more pessimistic connotations and was primarily associated with how to avoid real or perceived hazards'.

Significantly, as Giulianotti (2009) demonstrates, there are two broad ways of defining risk (see also Beck, 1999: 23–26). First, there are some risk analysts that view risk in largely scientific, technical and objective terms. For instance, through the use of statistical inferences from empirical data in order to estimate probabilities of future events (Jennings, 2012a). These understandings of risk often concern themselves with those uncertainties that may be objectively measured or quantified. Second, other existing definitions or comprehensions of risks 'highlight the social construction of risks relative to discourses, policies, sociohistorical processes and hegemonic forces' (Giulianotti, 2009: 541). Between these 'objective-natural and socially-constructed' (Domingues, 2021:4) comprehensions of risk, one would, for example, be able to position Beck's (1992: 21, original emphasis) influential understanding of risk as 'a systematic way of dealing with hazards and insecurities induced and introduced by modernization itself'. Giddens (1999: 3), meanwhile, asserts that a society 'increasingly preoccupied with the future (and also with safety)' has generated the notion of risk. Essentially, Beck's hybrid critical realist-constructivist approach implies that 'risks are both objectively real and socially constructed' (Clapton, 2011: 282; see also Lupton, 1999). Concerning the latter, this speaks to how modernity has rationalized the notion of 'risk' – as compared to earlier civilizations – but still, 'it cannot always be expressed in percentages and maths' (Domingues, 2022: 8). Notwithstanding, Giulianotti (2009: 551) reminds us that there are 'beneficial consequences' of Beck's 'dual focus' since this has advanced social sciences beyond realist and positivist risk epistemologies. For the remainder of this book, I principally approach risk in a modern and social constructivist manner. Importantly, this does not translate into a rejection of objective risks. Rather, it means that the book is predominantly concerned with the socio-cultural processes through which risks are mediated, practiced, perceived or constructed.

Risk can be considered a 'quintessentially modern construct; that is, risk calculations guide particular human interventions within contexts of generalized uncertainty' (Giulianotti, 2009: 541). Here, the notion of interventions in uncertainty packed contexts remains important to emphasize because this implies that future risks cannot, in fact, always be avoided or mitigated. Ultimately, relevant interventions do not always nor necessarily *minimize* risks, or those social anxieties associated with them. Rather, interventions may solely serve to elevate our awareness and anxieties of risks even further, because: 'Risk meanings and strategies are attempts to tame uncertainty, but often have the paradoxical effect of increasing anxiety about risk through the intensity of their focus and concern' (Lupton, 1999: 13). Indeed, here rests one of the central paradoxes of risk, its management and meanings which, as I shall demonstrate, is highly transferable to and identifiable within contemporary and global football contexts.

Risky games? Research on risk, sport and football: a brief overview

This section briefly reviews the pre-existing research on risk in sport yet focuses chiefly on football. It would be unfair to argue that researchers interested in sport are yet to academically engage with risk, risk assessments or management in sport or football. However, given the aforementioned and pronounced prominence of risk in the public life and in academic spheres over the last 30 years, it remains surprising that the linkages between modern risks and football have been somewhat overlooked in the literature. In the sociology of sport, risk analysis and frameworks have been employed, but primarily in the 'investigation of particular topics' (Giulianotti, 2009: 540). Following Giulianotti's (2009) directions, there are particularly four broad ways of theorizing risk in sport, including (1) risk and calculation; (2) hedonism, voluntarism and transcendence; (3) risk cultures and subcultures in sport; and finally, (4) the links between risk and modernization. Along these lines, the book predominantly remains concerned with the latter.

In relation to voluntarism, transcendence and risk cultures, there is, for example, a sizable body of research on voluntary risk-taking in sport, or 'edgework', as it is commonly theorized as (Lyng, 2005). Here, researchers have been primarily concerned with understanding the participants' meanings and motives for participating in extremely risky sports or leisure activities. Some examples include BASE jumping, skydiving or Mixed Martial Arts: sporting activities that may cause serious injury or even death but that also generate, for participants, a feeling of sensation, thrill and a break from the mundanity of 'everyday' routines (Kidder, 2022). Some academic studies on 'hooliganism' can also be positioned within this area of research.

For instance, scholars have explored why individuals participate in football-related violence which can involve a great deal of physical risks for participants (Finn, 1994).

Concerning the nucleus between risk and football, some scholars have explored the risks of injury that elite footballers are exposed to. Fuller et al. (2012), for example, look at *Fédération Internationale de Football Association's* (FIFA) modes of risk management for the mitigation and communication of injury risks. Then, notably, there is a growing body of literature dealing with risk management, perceptions or communication at sporting events or in specific football contexts (Cleland, 2019; Lee Ludvigsen, 2020; Lee Ludvigsen and Parnell, 2021; Toohey, 2008; Spaaij, 2013; Jennings, 2012a, 2012b; Leopkey and Parent, 2009). Leopkey and Parent (2009) break down the diverse risk categories at major sporting events faced by stakeholders and organizing committees, whereas Toohey (2008) and Cleland (2019) deploy Beck's (1992) ideas to explore how sport events, organizations and spectators have responded to the heightened terrorist threats in a globalized epoch, as a trend identifiable both on the inside and outside of major sport events. Significantly, based on the voices of sport fans, Cleland (2019: 150) argues that the 'risk society [...] is present in the minds of a significant number of fans across a variety of sports' with fans displaying both an awareness and consciousness of risks related to sport event attendance. Such argument, of course, remains highly influential for this book, which seeks to build upon such contention.

Moreover, in Lee Ludvigsen (2022), I explored how Covid-19 transitioned from a 'risk' to a concrete 'threat' in sport in the spring of 2020, and how sport governing bodies communicated their adherence to the World Health Organization's (WHO) guidelines, as the scientific 'expert system' in the start of the pandemic crisis. Also situated in the political and social scientific literature, which is of primary relevance here, Jennings's (2012a) *Olympic Risks* marks a significant contribution. Jennings explores, *inter alia*, financial risks, decision-making, reputational risks and public opinion, risk management and the costs/benefits of the Olympic Games. Whilst Jennings successfully demonstrates that diverse risks and their management lie at the heart of Olympic projects, his book does not (and does not intend to) focus specifically on risks in football.[2] However, Jennings's work still confirms that sport *is* a field ready for risk-informed investigation and analysis. As he argues elsewhere:

> Mega-events such as the Olympic Games present a special case for understanding the relationship between large-scale projects and

societal and institutional risks, and how these in turn give rise to pressures for the management of risk.

(Jennings, 2012b: 2)

This quote clearly suggests that sports-related contexts (i.e., the Olympics) hold a special relevance and remain important for the social study of risk. This proposition, I argue, resonates with and is transferable to football contexts, such as football mega-events like the World Cup, transnational tournaments like the Champions League or professional domestic leagues. Notwithstanding, as stressed earlier, there is still a scholarly need for further research on risks in sport (cf. Giulianotti, 2009). Within this unfilled space, it can be argued that the *implications of global risk societies on football* remain ready for further academic engagement and analysis.

This book: approach and chapters

This short book examines global risks situated across football. Still, I concur with Cleland (2015: 4–5) who acknowledged that: 'No book can cover every aspect of football in every place in the world'. Importantly, and partly due to space restrictions, it is impossible for this book to cover – or even pretend to cover – *all* global risks that may be located across *all* regions of the world. Yet perhaps as important: that is not my intention either. So, cases and mini case studies are primarily drawn from British and European football contexts, and from past and future World Cup editions hosted outside Europe. The book concentrates mainly on those major international championships; the football mega-events that represent 'global spectacles' and other top professional leagues operating within the relational and networked 'Football Worlds' (Parnell et al., 2021) and 'global football field' (Giulianotti and Robertson, 2012). Naturally, this concentration may be viewed as a serious omission. Though, simultaneously, as Chapter 6 acknowledges, those directions I provide apply to football contexts that are not confined to those which I explore throughout this book. Furthermore, the selection of those risk exemplars and cases I provide can be justified since they are among the most central and pressing risk-related issues in football and society more widely (i.e., violence, political risks, the environment, the media) and because they best assist the aim of showcasing and exemplifying the broader risks that this book is concerned with.

Then, throughout this book, my approach is mainly conceptual. As such, I draw upon and borrow from a range of interdisciplinary literatures and emerging perspectives that underpin my analysis. This includes the mainstream sociological and the sociology of sport literatures (Chapter 2). Yet, I also borrow existing insights from criminology (Chapters 4 and 5) and hence this book also consciously slides into, and situates itself within, the emerging critical criminology of sport project which fundamentally seeks to engage with topics such as 'crime', 'risk' and 'social control' across sport (Groombridge, 2017; Millward et al., in press).

Thus, in order to work towards the book's aims and to inform my arguments, I draw substantially from traditional secondary sources in form of published academic literature, whilst also utilizing media sources, websites, interviews conducted by newspapers/journalists (Chapter 5) and analyzes of publicly available policy documents such as World Cup bidding documents, reports and executive summaries (Chapter 3).

***

The book is divided into six chapters including this introduction. Both collectively and individually, these chapters will sharpen the contours of my already hinted upon main argument which maintains that football reveals many of the key characteristics of global risk societies and could be positioned at the forefront of our understanding of risk and the socio-cultural changes occurring in risk societies (cf. Beck, 1992). Notwithstanding, to fully grasp such argument, a theoretical and conceptual sociological introduction is necessary. So, Chapter 2 outlines this book's key theoretical and conceptual touchstones. Here, I first unpack the concept of 'globalization' with a particular reference to football. Then, the chapter discusses perspectives on risk advanced by Beck and Giddens and, finally, on 'governmentality' and risk as inspired by Foucault's writings. Having erected a theoretically informed scaffold, this chapter concludes by arguing for an increased scholarly appreciation of the *football/risk/globalization* triangle.

Chapter 3 will investigate the global politics of the environment in football. It examines the intertwined environmental and political risks that can arise around the quadrennial FIFA men's World Cup. Whereas an old saying maintains that 'sport and politics should not mix' (Power et al., 2020: 1), the reality is that sport (particularly so, football) and politics do indeed mix. This will be exemplified here by the so-called 'greening' of World Cup legacies (Death, 2011) and 'anti-mega-event' protests serving as indicators of, first, institutional reflexivity in football and, second, the potential political backlashes of countries' World Cup housing. Chapter 4 then weaves together existing insights on how football supporters in the present-day are governed through risk. By borrowing and advancing contemporary concepts from criminology and criminal justice, including Zedner's (2007) concept of 'pre-crime', it explores the mechanisms through which fans across Europe are routinely classified according to the alleged 'risk' they pose and how the anticipation of *future* football-related violence or disorder commonly means that national and sporting authorities turn towards new pre-emptive technologies of surveillance. As argued, this risk management aspect comprises a concretized, perpetually evolving yet resisted aspect of football's (risk) cultures. This, however, must be considered sociologically and criminologically important, because it informs our understanding of the wider significance of risk projects, technology and culture in the present-day.

Then, given that one of the key tenets of the risk society is an enhanced awareness of risks on an individual level (Beck, 1992; Cleland, 2019), Chapter 5 examines how football supporters perceive risks, fear and insecurity in relation to football events. While establishing safety and minimizing risks remain two rationales behind risk management and security procedures at football mega-events (Lee Ludvigsen, 2020) and one-off fixtures, little is known – theoretically and empirically – about what fans feel about risks and how they negotiate heightened risk. Do fans feel afraid, anxious, safe or resilient when attending crowded football events? Additionally, the chapter pays attention to how risk is communicated *through* or *by* the media in an epoch where themes like fear and risk are intensely mediated before sporting events (Atkinson and Young, 2012). This is exemplified by a case study of the English Premier League's 'Project Restart' during the first UK Covid-19 lockdown in the spring of 2020. In closing, Chapter 6 summarizes the book's arguments and conclusions while it reflects on the directions for future theoretical and empirical work on risk *in* and *beyond* football.

Notes

1 See Lupton (1999: 5–12) for a longer historical account of the term 'risk'.
2 Although football, of course, features as one Olympic sport.

References

Aradau, C., Lobo-Guerro, L. and Van Munster, R. (2008) 'Security, Technologies of Risk, and the Political: Guest Editors' Introduction', *Security Dialogue* 39(2–3): 147–154.

Atkinson, M. and Young, K. (2012) 'Shadowed by the Corpse of War: Sport Spectacles and the Spirit of Terrorism', *International Review for the Sociology of Sport* 47(3): 286–306.

Beck, U. (1992) *Risk Society: Towards a New Modernity*, London: Sage.

Beck, U. (1999) *World Risk Society*, Cambridge: Polity Press.

Clapton, W. (2011) 'Risk in International Relations', *International Relations* 25(3): 280–295.

Cleland, J. (2015) *A Sociology of Football in a Global Context*, London: Routledge.

Cleland, J. (2019) 'Sports Fandom in the Risk Society: Analyzing Perceptions and Experiences of Risk, Security and Terrorism at Elite Sports Events', *Sociology of Sport Journal* 36(2): 144–151.

Death, C. (2011) '"Greening" the 2010 FIFA World Cup: Environmental Sustainability and the Mega-Event in South Africa', *Journal of Environmental Policy & Planning* 13(2): 99–117.

Domingues, J.M. (2022) 'From Global Risk to Global Threat: State Capabilities and Modernity in Times of Coronavirus', *Current Sociology* 70(1): 6–23.

Domingues, J.M. (2021) 'Climate Change and Its Lexicon: An Analytical and Critical View', *International Journal of Politics, Culture, and Society*: 1–16.

Finn, G.P.T. (1994) 'Football Violence: A Societal Psychological Perspective', *Football Violence and Social Identity* (Eds. R. Giulianotti, N. Bonney and M. Hepworth), London: Routledge, pp. 90–127.

Fuller, C.W., Junge, A. and Dvorak, J. (2012) 'Risk Management: FIFA's Approach for Protecting the Health of Football Players', *British Journal of Sports Medicine* 46(1): 11–17.

Giddens, A. (1999) 'Risk and Responsibility', *The Modern Law Review* 62(1): 1–35.

Giulianotti, R. (2009) 'Risk and Sport: An Analysis of Sociological Theories and Research Agendas', *Sociology of Sport Journal* 26(4): 540–556.

Giulianotti, R. and Robertson, R. (2009) *Globalization and Football*, London: Sage.

Giulianotti, R. and Robertson, R. (2012) 'Mapping the Global Football Field: A Sociological Model of Transnational Forces within the World Game', *The British Journal of Sociology* 63(2): 216–240.

Groombridge, N. (2017) *Sports Criminology: A Critical Criminology of Sport and Games*, Policy: Bristol.

Jennings, W. (2012a) *Olympic Risks*, Basingstoke: Palgrave.

Jennings, W. (2012b) 'Mega-Events and Risk Colonisation: Risk Management and the Olympics', *Discussion Paper No. 71*, London: London School of Economics and Political Science.

Kidder, J.L. (2021) 'Reconsidering Edgework Theory: Practices, Experiences, and Structures', *International Review for the Sociology of Sport* 57(2): 183–200.

Lee Ludvigsen, J.A. (2020) 'The "Troika of Security": Merging Retrospective and Futuristic 'Risk' and 'Security' Assessments before Euro 2020', *Leisure Studies* 39(6): 844–858.

Lee Ludvigsen, J.A. (2022) 'When "The Show" Cannot Go on: An Investigation into Sports Mega-Events and Responses during the Pandemic Crisis', *International Review for the Sociology of Sport* 57(4): 497–514.

Lee Ludvigsen, J.A. and Parnell, D. (2021) 'Redesigning the Games? The 2020 Olympic Games, Playbooks and New Sports Event Risk Management Tools', *Managing Sport and Leisure*: 1–13.

Leopkey, B. and Parent, M.M. (2009) 'Risk Management Issues in Large-Scale Sporting Events: A Stakeholder Perspective', *European Sport Management Quarterly* 9(2): 187–208.

Lupton, D. (1999) *Risk*, London: Routledge.

Lyng, S. (eds.) (2005) *Edgework: The Sociology of Risk Taking*, New York/London: Routledge.

Millward, P. (2011) *The Global Football League: Transnational Networks, Social Movements and Sport in the New Media Age*, Basingstoke: Palgrave.

Millward, P., Lee Ludvigsen, J.A. and Sly, J. (in press) *Sport and Crime: Towards a Critical Criminology of Sport*, Routledge.

Mythen, G. (2004) *Ulrich Beck: A Critical Introduction to the Risk Society*, London: Pluto Press.

Parnell, D., Bond, A.J., Widdop, P. and Cockayne, D. (2021) 'Football Worlds: Business and Networks during COVID-19', *Soccer & Society* 22(1–2): 19–26.

Power, M.J., Widdop, P., Parnell, D., Carr, J. and Millar, S.R. (2020) 'Football and Politics: The Politics of Football', *Managing Sport and Leisure* 25(1–2): 1–5.

Spaaij, R. (2013) 'Risk, Security and Technology: Governing Football Supporters in the Twenty-First Century', *Sport in Society* 16(2): 167–183.

Toohey, K. (2008) 'Terrorism, Sport and Public Policy in the Risk Society', *Sport in Society* 11(4): 429–442.

Tooze, A. (2020) 'The Sociologist Who Could Save Us from Coronavirus', *Foreign Policy*, available from: https://foreignpolicy.com/2020/08/01/the-sociologist-who-could-save-us-from-coronavirus/.

Weimer, M. (2017) 'The Origins of "Risk" as an Idea and the Future of Risk Regulation', *European Journal of Risk Regulation* 8(1): 10–17.

Zedner, L. (2007) 'Pre-Crime and Post-Criminology?', *Theoretical Criminology* 11(2): 261–281.

Zinn, J. (2009) 'The Sociology of Risk and Uncertainty: Current State and Perspectives', *The Future of Sociology* (Eds. S. Lockie, D. Bissell, A. Greig, M. Hynes, D. Marsh, L. Saha, J. Sikora and D. Woodman), Australian Sociological Association, pp. 1–14.

2 Globalization, Theorizing Risk and the Risk Society

Introduction

By building on Chapter 1, this chapter will introduce, map out and discuss the key theoretical tools and sociological understandings of risk with a special orientation towards Beck's (1992) influential 'risk society' thesis. However, given the central importance of 'de-localized' and 'global' risks in the (world) risk society (see Beck, 1999), the chapter also provides an account of 'globalization' which simultaneously represents one of the key concepts in both the mainstream social sciences and the social study of football. This account will assist our understanding of *why* certain risks could be considered 'global' and, indeed, why professional football is commonly viewed as a 'global game' that reflects the core characteristics of globalization processes. Importantly, whereas scholars have appreciated the importance and impact of globalization processes on football (and, *in reverse*, football's influence on globalization processes) (e.g., Cleland, 2015; Giulianotti and Robertson, 2004; Millward, 2011), this chapter – drawing upon this literature – argues that one illuminating field for further investigation is the intersecting triad of globalization, risk and football. Both in separation and collectively, I argue, these three areas remain relevant for our understanding of wider sociological problems. Therefore, a contemporary and critical engagement with the *inter-connections* between the three remains important because it allows for appraising their more general and dynamic co-existence and for analyzing social transformations that have pierced through football as one highly significant form of popular culture.

Structurally, this chapter will begin by defining and unpacking globalization and its applications to football. Next, it discusses the aforementioned risk society perspective and 'reflexive modernization' as two concepts most commonly associated with Ulrich Beck and

DOI: 10.4324/9781003303480-2

Anthony Giddens. In particular, the chapter highlights three key pillars of the risk society speaking to modern risk's (i) spatial/temporal diffuse, (ii) catastrophic and unpredictable and (iii) uncontrollable nature (see Mythen and Walklate, 2008). Finally, the chapter unpacks another perspective, that is 'governmentality', deriving from the writings of Michel Foucault (1991). After discussing this perspective's relation to risk, the chapter concludes by restating the relevance of this theoretical palette and its lenses through which football may be viewed, as the book proceeds.

Unpacking globalization

To fully grasp why several of those football-related risks discussed in this book can be considered 'global' in their nature and scope, it is necessary to better understand what 'globalization' is, as one of the keys and repeated themes throughout this book. However, much like the term 'risk', the deployment and study of the term 'globalization' have expanded massively over the previous three decades (Albrow, 1996; Beck, 2000; Robertson, 1992). Since the 1990s, globalization has become one of the main themes – if not *the* main theme – of the social sciences (Millward, 2011). Whilst we, simply put, have witnessed a 'global turn' in the social sciences (Giulianotti and Robertson, 2009: xii), globalization is concurrently a highly contested concept with varying and diverse meanings and theorizations. Naturally, this makes it prudent to ask questions about what exactly globalization is (cf. Beck, 2000), and whether it might be more appropriate to speak of 'globalizations' as plural processes, rather than one single process (Robertson and White, 2007).

Following sociologist Roland Robertson (1992: 8), globalization is a concept that may be defined as 'the compression of the world and the intensification of consciousness of the world as a whole'. As facilitated much by intensified communication on a transnational level, as assisted by technological progress, this comprehension of 'globalization' simultaneously captures the idea of the world as an increasingly compressed and singular place (Giulianotti, 2016). Beck (2000: 11, original emphasis), meanwhile, highlighted that '*globalization* [...] denotes the *processes* through which sovereign national states are criss-crossed and undermined by transnational actors with varying prospects of power, orientations, identities and networks'. Following this, globalization processes and the (inter-connected) rise of transnational corporations and international organizations have challenged and eroded the traditional nation-state's roles and positions.

Ultimately, at the very core of globalization lies worldwide transformation and social changes. Unevenly, these have taken place across political social, economic and cultural domains across the globe (Lee Ludvigsen, 2020). Despite this, it remains important to highlight that:

> Most significantly globalization has been strongly associated with capitalist power, seeing certain states and corporations controlling world markets. A social and cultural homogenization marked by the universalization of particular, dominant centres such as 'The West' or 'America' are often depicted in rather dystopic ways as the real consequences of these influences.
>
> (Hognestad, 2009: 361)

This reminder connects with Castells's (2000) argument that globalization discourses are traceable to notions of economic transnationalism which lie at the nucleus of the flows of people, information and images across the globe in the epoch of intensified globalization. Essentially, given the rise of transnational economies and capitalist markets across sport, and the fact that sport has undergone powerful globalization processes, the body of literature on globalization, sport and football has grown considerably over the last two decades, as the next section throws a light on.

The global game: globalization and football

In the present-day, football can be – and regularly is – described and analytically approached as a highly 'global game' (Giulianotti, 1999; Horne and Jary, 2004) and indeed a 'global business'. Cleland elaborates on this:

> Football has become a global business that is based on transnational corporatisation and brand expansion, not only for the many corporate organisations now involved in the global game but also for the elite clubs that participate in it. This has been helped by the neo-liberal nature of football since the 1990s, most notably through satellite television and the broadcasting of domestic, continental, and international football all over the world.
>
> (Cleland, 2015: 1)

Consequently, several scholars have, in illuminating fashion, examined the various direct and indirect consequences and impacts of globalization in football (and other sports, too). As such, it is fair to claim that the study of globalization in sport has substantially assisted our wider and more 'mainstream' sociological understanding of globalization (e.g., Bairner, 2001; Cleland, 2015; Doidge, 2015; Giulianotti and Robertson, 2004, 2007, 2009; Millward, 2011). At the same time, globalization should not automatically be viewed as a set of processes that have been 'externally imposed upon the game' – rather, football should be approached as one important manifestation of globalization (Giulianotti and Robertson, 2004: 546). Indeed, Foer (2005) even suggests that football – more than anything else in societies – has the capacity to explain the consequences of globalization on societies.

By taking a socio-historical approach, Giulianotti and Robertson (2009) devise a five-phased model of football's globalization in their influential work.[1] Their analytical model has its starting point in the early fifteenth century and ends in the early 2000s. Notwithstanding, they also tentatively advance the sixth phase: the *millennial phase* (which commenced in the early 2000s and continues onwards). Within an overarching globalization frame, it is primarily this socio-temporal 'millennial phase' that this book's subsequent chapters – and the issues discussed within these – are situated within. This phase emerged following the 9/11 attacks and resembles a risk society insofar it is defined by the 'generalized spread and darkening of climates of fear across socio-cultural realms' demonstrated by more pronounced anxieties regarding personal security, national identity and the global environment (ibid.: 27). However, even in 2009, the authors acknowledged that this phase was still in its 'preliminary stages' (ibid.: 28). In itself, this is crucial insofar as it provides an additional rationale for understanding better how this phase has advanced further and continued to influence football and, moreover, how this phase fits under the risk society's wide umbrella (see Kossakowski, 2014).

Ultimately, a scan over the existing reservoir of research on globalization in football shows that the areas that have been covered include *inter alia* the 'clashes' between local and global forces (Armstrong and Mitchell, 2008; Duke, 2002), the impacts on football's fandom (Millward, 2011; Nash, 2000; Petersen-Wagner, 2017), consumption, media and broadcasting (David and Millward, 2012; Sandvoss, 2003), neoliberalism and emerging global and networked markets (Cleland, 2015; Lee Ludvigsen and Millward, 2019). Though, a similar scan reveals that minimal research examines the intersections between globalization and risk in football. That is despite the fact that it has been argued that there has been a 'risk turn' in social sciences, in a similar fashion to, and coinciding with, the mentioned 'global turn' (Giulianotti, 2009). Indeed, Jennings sheds a light on the interconnections between risk and globalization, maintaining that:

> Globalisation in its various forms exacerbates the interconnectedness of risk (transmitted through global telecommunication and supply networks, international travel, migration and crossborder movement of goods, services and capital), while technological and scientific innovation also create opportunities for the inadvertent production of risk. These processes accelerate the contagion of risk, such as in the form of pandemic disease or shocks to the financial markets.
>
> (Jennings, 2012: 4)

Following this, globalization processes facilitate the spread of risks on a global level as the interconnectedness between societies, individuals and cultures increases. And, ultimately, the risk society that is discussed next can be located within the 'second modernity' which is 'increasingly disaggregated, globalized, reflexive and uncertain' (Giulianotti, 2009: 550). This period has seen enormous social transformations and had far-reaching consequences for political orders, social institutions, global policies and has fundamentally come to guide the social organization of individuals' lives.

The risk society: Beck, Giddens and the reflexive modernity

Broadly, both Ulrich Beck and Anthony Giddens shared the view that risk is *the* central issue of the contemporary times, and that this conundrum was induced by processes attributed to modernization. The German sociologist, Ulrich Beck, is seen by many as one of the most prominent sociological thinkers of our age (see Mythen, 2005). To date, his risk society perspective remains one of the most influential theses and theoretical works in the contemporary lexicon on risk within the social sciences. Beck's risk society theory was first featured in the German edition, *Risikogesellschaft*, published in 1986 (see also Beck, 1987). A few years later, the English-translated version *Risk Society: Towards a New Modernity* (1992) was published and consequently became a catalyst for intensified debates about the nature of risk in modern western societies (Lupton, 1999). The work has been described as one of the 'most ambitious and provocative texts written within the social sciences in recent years' (Mythen, 2004: 11) and following the publication of his landmark text, Beck extended his thesis and continued to write on risk and revisit his work over the next years (see, e.g., Beck, 1999, 2002, 2016: Ch. 5). This included, for instance, the publication of *World Risk Society* (1999) and his reflections on the 9/11 attacks in the USA and how the latter, in a way, exemplified the 'world risk society' and the shortcomings of rational risk calculations in times of uncontrollable risk (Beck, 2002).

At the core, Beck's (1992) diagnosis of the evolving social conditions was concerned with how risks and hazards have changed between the pre-industrial, industrial and modern societies. In line with modernization processes and especially the innovations, advances and activities within the realms of science and technology, Beck argued that we have entered a new phase – the risk society – which became discernible from the 1970s and onwards (Burgess et al., 2018). In a way, the shift from industrial (or class) societies towards risk societies is illustrated by the following quote:

> [T]he driving force in the class society can be summarized in the phrase: *I am hungry!* The movement set in motion by the risk society, on the other hand, is expressed in the statement: *I am afraid!* The commonality of anxiety takes the place of the commonality of need.
>
> (Beck, 1992: 49, original emphasis)

The risk society is a society increasingly aware of, organized around and preoccupied with the management and minimization of risk and hazards that – to a larger extent than before – are 'man-made' or 'manufactured'. Such risks may be juxtaposed to the hazards characterizing the industrial societies that, whilst dangerous, remained relatively naturally occurring and geographically constrained.

As Beck himself noted, risks, which are contrasted by older dangers, 'are consequences which relate to the threatening force of modernization, and to its globalization of doubt. They are *politically reflexive*' (1992: 21, original emphasis). Essentially, the typical man-made risks and hazards can be linked to intensifying globalizing forces, mobilities, capitalist markets and technological interventions. They include, for example, toxic waste, radiation leaks, pollution, hazards stemming from scientific or technological experiments and terrorism, financial crashes and even the global spread of infectious diseases like HIV/AIDS (Giulianotti, 2016; Jennings, 2012) or Covid-19 (Wardman and Lofstedt, 2020). And crucially, as Chapters 3–6 discuss, many of these risks and their impacts are highly identifiable in football. Furthermore, these manufactured risks are induced by the practices of 'people, firms, state agencies and politicians' (Beck, 1992: 98). Risk has essentially emerged as *the* defining feature of the new phase of society, and thus Beck (2006: 330) contended that: 'Being at risk is the way of being and ruling in the world of modernity; being at global risk is the human condition at the beginning of the twenty-first century'.

Following Beck (1992) and Beck et al. (1994), this phase or epoch can be understood as 'reflexive modernization'. This is where the unintended and unpredictable consequences of modernity begin to play out. The reflexive modernity is characterized by the erosion of traditional institutions and, as a result, risk awareness and uncertainty escalated across societies. For example, individuals spend more time contemplating future risks than in previous eras. As Ekberg (2007) writes:

> by an increase in attempts to colonize and control the near and distant future [...] reflexive modernity is characterized by an awareness of living in a society of increasing vulnerability to the unpredictable, unfamiliar and unprecedented risks manufactured by modern science and technology.
>
> (ibid.: 345)

The idea of increased vulnerability has profound impacts on a societal level. As Lupton (1999: 59) summarizes, '[t]he central problem of western societies, therefore, is not the production and distributions of "goods" such as wealth and employment in conditions of scarcity [...] but the prevention or minimization of "bads"; that is, risks', including but not limited to the mentioned environmental devastation, nuclear incidents, transnational terrorism or infectious diseases. Importantly here, this is partly due to the globalization processes and interconnected *universal* nature of risks and hazards (Giulianotti, 2009). Hence, where the 'logic of the class society is sectoral – some win and some lose', Mythen and Walklate (2008: 224) observe that, 'the logic of the risk society is universal – everyone loses', even the wealthy and powerful profiteers of risk.

The risk society may be neatly summarized as 'a society in which there are uncontrollable and unpredictable dangers against which insurance is impossible' (Aradau and Van Munster, 2007: 90). Such concise summary largely echoes Mythen and Walklate's (2008) reading of the risk society as underpinned by primarily *three* key pillars that are now broken down. First, that is the greater 'temporal and spatial' mobility of risks. Risks and hazards are no longer confined geographically nor temporally. Instead, risks increasingly operate on a global scale – as evidenced by, for instance, the 1986 Chernobyl disaster and transnational terrorist attacks such as the aforementioned 9/11.[2] Second, another pillar of the risk society is the enormous potential harm that is inherent to several global risks that 'generate irremediable effects' (ibid.: 224). This speaks especially to technological and scientific activities or interventions that intensify the potentially *existential* threat and catastrophic nature of risks. Third, the last key pillar relates to the mentioned 'manufactured' or 'man-made' hazards and dangers of the risk society which shatter the 'extant methods of insurance' (ibid.). In other words, in (world) risk societies, there are visible and invisible risks that fundamentally *cannot* be managed, controlled or insured against through pre-existing formulas, calculations or acquired knowledge. Under such conditions, social institutions are consequently unable to provide or guarantee public safety (Mythen, 2004), which citizens have become increasingly reflexive and conscious about (Giulianotti, 2009). This again has contributed towards an 'increasingly active mistrust of corporations, scientific institutions and government' (Burgess et al., 2018: 2).

For Beck, as Chapter 1 mentioned, the omnipresent risks remain real – in an objective and realist sense – but are *simultaneously* marked by a social construction. The latter is much due to citizens' reflexivity and heightened awareness or perceptions of specific risks. As he wrote, risks can be 'magnified, dramatized or minimized' and are hence 'open to social definition and construction' (Beck, 1992: 23, original emphasis). Thus, as an example, the mass media's communications of risk may serve to enhance or define specific risks' 'social and political positions' (ibid.; see Chapter 5). In his later writings, Beck elaborated on this. For instance, he developed the concept of 'staging', explaining how risk and potential crises are socially staged through mass mediation (Beck, 2009). Though, staging can also accelerate the eventual political responses to potential future catastrophes that have become publicly defined. Staging, therefore, is an 'attempt to publicly play out future risks through processes of pre-visualization' (Mythen, 2018: 22). The mass media therefore ensures the *visibility* of risks: 'It is only through mediated images that [global risks] acquire the power to break through [their] invisibility' (Beck, 2016: 127). Then, one of the real paradoxes of risk is that the solutions for the management of contingency 'often also have the effect of increasing anxiety about risk through their constant focus upon catastrophic and dystopic imaginations of the future' (Aradau et al., 2008: 149).

Notwithstanding the widespread influence of Beck's risk theories in several social scientific fields over the last 30 years, his risk society thesis is – as argued in Chapter 1 – yet to be fully utilized in the sociologies of sport and football.[3] Further, Beck himself did not write specifically with reference to risks in sport or football. Significantly, however, that was not necessarily due to an absence of risk in the diverse realms of sport. As Giulianotti argues:

> In sport, Beck's analysis has had surprisingly little impact [...]
> For example, while athletes, officials and fans are more cognizant of the physical dangers and competitive iniquities of doping in sport, the enormous environmental costs of sport mega-events are rarely considered. Moreover, in developing nations, spectators and athletes endure relatively greater risks, such as bad stadium conditions, violent policing or crowd stampedes, weaker medical support for injuries, and (for professional sportspeople) the threat of unemployment.
>
> (Giulianotti, 2009: 551)

This remains pivotal as this book continues. Essentially, this quote reminds us of the presence and appearance of risks in football and sport more widely. Furthermore, whilst Beck's own work is yet to be fully embraced in the social study of football, the same may also be contended concerning the British sociologists Anthony Giddens's risk analyses, although Giddens's theoretical repertoire appears in, for example, Horne and Jary's (2004) chapter in the edited collection *Sport and Modern Social Theorists* (2004).[4]

Whilst the risk society was first developed by Beck, it was constructively developed further by Giddens (Horne and Jary, 2004). Like Beck, Giddens (1990, 1999a, 1999b; see also Beck et al., 1994) sees risk as a defining feature in the reflexive modernity. As Lupton's (1999) comparisons show, there are other distinctive convergences between Beck and Giddens' theorizations of risk. For example, on a macro-level, they both view risks as effects of human progress and, moreover, that lay people display a greater awareness of risk in late modernity (for further convergences, see Lupton, 1999: 72–83).

However, with regards to their differences, Lupton (1999) points out that Giddens does not contend that late modernity is characterized by *more* risks than in earlier epochs. For Giddens (1999a: 3), a risk society 'is not intrinsically more dangerous or hazardous than pre-existing forms of social order'. Rather, more subjectively, it is a case of a greater awareness being directed toward the risks from citizens (Lupton, 1999). Put another way, following Giddens, people are more sensitive to risks that they spend more time reflecting about. Moreover, on the concept of 'trust', the two also differ in the sense that Giddens argues that lay people's reflexivity is displayed by placing trust upon 'expert systems'. When anticipating risks, according to Giddens, individuals increasingly turn towards 'expert systems' who claim to possess expert knowledge on risks and to make risk judgements (ibid.). This pronounced turn toward 'expert knowledge' – which means that 'experts' (i.e., scientists, doctors, accountants) increasingly become 'gatekeepers of risk' (Hanlon, 2010: 214) – Beck remained far more critical of, particularly given the social construction of knowledge and scientific claims *vis-à-vis* 'objectivity' (Mythen, 2004). This renders the knowledge fields both extremely contested and open-ended (Hanlon, 2010) despite the façade of objectivity. Hence, in the Beckian view, the public approaches 'expert systems' more critically, as the *cause* of, and not merely the solution to wider problems (Giulianotti, 2016).

Ultimately, both Beck's and Giddens's theories on risk have been subject to criticism for appearing too speculative (Horne and Jary, 2004; Jarvis, 2007; Lupton, 1999).[5] For example, a common criticism of Beck's risk society thesis has been that it is 'empirically light' (Mythen, 2004: 183) or fails to acknowledge other important factors – beyond risk – in modern social and material life (Curran, 2016). Moreover, Beck's thesis has been 'interpreted by some as highly dystopic' (Mythen and Walklate, 2016: 407). Whilst acknowledging all this, there is little – if any – doubt that these insights remain hugely influential, relevant and thought-provoking in the sociological literature on risk; but also, as applied to other disciplines including international relations (Heng, 2006), security studies (Mythen and Walklate, 2016), criminology (Mythen and Walklate, 2006) and policing (Ericson and Haggerty, 1997). Importantly, however, my objective upon proceeding is not to 'theory-test' the above theoretical insights. Neither is my intention to impose them uncritically or forensically onto my forthcoming football-related discussions. Instead, these perspectives on how behaviours, policies and practices in societies are oriented and guided by a clearer risk awareness, and the three key pillars of the risk society (unpacked above), work as a *scaffold* and formulate a clear theoretically informed *filter* that this book and the forthcoming chapters can lean towards or be viewed through.

Governmentality and its relevance to risk

The chapter now turns to the inter-relationships between risk and governmentality theory. The concept of 'governmentality' is commonly associated with the French theorist and philosopher, Michel

Foucault, who introduced this term in his 1978 *Collége de France* lecture series to describe how institutions, forms of knowledge and techniques are used to exercise power over target populations (Lim, 2011). However, in fact, Foucault himself 'did not [...] purposively put risk at the heart of his project' (Mythen and Walklate, 2006: 384) and he did not write much with direct reference to the concept of risk in comparison to Beck and Giddens. Yet many of his ideas on governmentality and modernity have, more recently, been applied to socio-cultural analysis of risk and its management (Dean, 2010; Lupton, 1999).

'Governmentality' represents an approach to the social regulation and control of populations (Foucault, 1991). Through his historical analysis, Foucault (1991) showed how this emerged as a new form of power that embedded itself within social relations, practices and discourses. This emerging system of regulation, in contemporary societies, is principally concerned with the 'conduct of conduct' (Flynn, 2002). Broadly, the 'conduct of conduct' refers to how governmentality 'is about the disciplining and regulation of the population without direct or oppressive intervention' (ibid.: 163). Government, therefore, shapes a person's or group's conduct (Kelly, 2003). However, the government is not restricted to state apparatuses. Rather, it may be understood as the pluralized activities carried out by multiple authorities and agencies – assisted by different techniques – which seek 'to shape conduct by working through our desires, aspirations, interests and beliefs' (Dean, 1999: 11). Following Foucault then, when 'something has been governmentalized', he referred to the process where that 'something' has 'assumed a particular form and style of managing its subjects' (Lim, 2011: 16).

Since the eighteenth century, Foucault argued, 'governmentality' had become a feature of political power (Mythen and Walklate, 2006). Accordingly, European states started to approach their citizens 'in terms of populations, or "society", a social body requiring intervention, management and protection as to maximize wealth, welfare and productivity' (Lupton, 1999: 85–86). Significantly, this contrasted the earlier imaginations of European government based on the core principles of legitimate rule (ibid.; Kelly, 2003) where power traditionally was 'expressed through the direct will of sovereign monarchs' (Mythen and Walklate, 2006: 384).

However, a natural question is, as Mythen and Walklate (2006: 384) ask: 'But how does all this relate to risk?'. One answer is that, following the governmentality perspective, *risk* becomes one specific mode of control and regulation. As Lupton explains:

According to the Foucauldian perspective, risk strategies and discourses are means of ordering the social and material worlds through methods of rationalization and calculation, attempts to render disorder and uncertainty more controllable. It is these strategies and discourses that bring risk into being, that select certain phenomena as being 'risky' and therefore requiring management, either by institutions or individuals.

(Lupton, 1999: 102)

Following this perspective, individuals are no longer approached in a holistic manner. Instead, they carry indicators which demonstrate their affiliation to, for example, 'at risk' or 'risky' groups that require intervention or regulation (Zinn and Taylor-Gooby, 2006). In this book's context, this carries a clear relevance to football-related settings (Chapters 4 and 5). As Giulianotti (2009) writes, the governmentality theory that can be extracted from Foucault's writings alludes particularly to the technologies of the state, which represent technologies of power. Ultimately, governmentality theory 'charts the exercise of power across populations, notably in the definition and clustering of individuals according to impersonal probability calculations' (ibid.: 543). For instance, this becomes visible through how law enforcement agencies or security professionals classify specific tournaments, football games or individuals as 'high-risk' according to 'particular "risk" characteristics (e.g., most likely to cause disturbances, most likely to be drawn into disturbances)' (ibid.; see also Chapter 4). Or, indeed, the all-seated stadiums that are surveilled by stadium officers and CCTV cameras which collectively restrict crowds' freedom of movement (Giulianotti, 2016: 120). Though, overall, the Foucauldian approaches to risk are characterized by a far more distinct social constructivist approach to the power relations that emerge around 'risk', its discourses and designated 'risk' populations (Lupton, 1999).

Conclusion

In arguing that the dynamic intersections between globalization, risk and football warrant further critical engagement, this chapter has principally focused on unpacking globalization and contemporary sociological perspectives on risk. More specifically, it has contextualized football as a sport and industry that is considered to be highly 'global' and engaged with the theoretical insights on risk influenced directly or indirectly by Beck and Giddens and, lastly, Foucault. Essentially, this discussion has elucidated the contention that '[i]n terms of theory,

Foucault and Beck provide the most sophisticated and stimulating work on risk for sociologists of sport' (Giulianotti, 2009: 552). In terms of the risk society thesis, unpacked above, this remains principally focused on the 'catalytic effects of risk on social transformation' (Mythen and Walklate, 2016: 404). This remains crucial, because in such societies, risks are increasingly uncontrollable, unpredictable and transnational in their scope.

The rationale for this chapter was to provide the relevant conceptual lenses and theoretical touchstones for the forthcoming chapters that focus more directly on global risks and their management, which may be situated at the frontiers of contemporary elite football. Football has not been isolated nor left untouched from the social transformations described above, which have seen risks become increasingly de-localized and global (Houlihan and Giulianotti, 2012). However, the key argument of this chapter must be seen against the backdrop of the fact that football and sport, over the last 20 years, have functioned as rich and illuminating sites for scholarly analyses of globalization (Cleland, 2015; Giulianotti and Robertson, 2009; Millward, 2011). In fact, it has been contended that 'sport, and especially football, is epicentral to contemporary globalization processes' (Giulianotti and Robertson, 2004: 561). Notwithstanding, as this chapter argues, considering the direct and indirect connections between sociological risk theories in modern societies and globalization (Heng, 2006; Jarvis, 2007), one prominent research gap that surfaces speak directly to the need for further critical examinations of the global risk societies' impact on present-day football, as an important social, political, economic and cultural institution of modern societies (Giulianotti, 1999). *Prima facie*, professional football appears to possess the potential for seriously supplementing our understanding of the globalization of risk. Importantly then, a further analysis and a reconsideration of football are both required. Significantly, this informs this book's underlying aims, which were stated in Chapter 1. To reiterate, these were, first, to showcase how football serves as an illuminating site for the global risks that are situated in modern societies. Second, to (-re-)energize and provide directions for the field of risk analysis in football.

Notes

1 These include the (1 & 2) germinal and incipient phases up to the 1870s; (3) the take-off phase (1870s–mid-1920s); (4) the 'struggle-for-hegemony' phase (mid-1920s–late 1960s) and finally, (5) the uncertainty phase (late 1960s to 2000) (see Giulianotti and Robertson, 2009, Ch. 1).

2 The Chernobyl disaster in fact coincided with the original publication of the risk society (see Beck (1987) for his reflections).
3 Exceptions include e.g., Giulianotti (2009) and Cleland (2015). A few other applications of Beck's work to football exist: Petersen-Wagner's (2019) uses Beck's work on 'individualization' in his fascinating study of Liverpool FC fans, traditions and solidarities. Kossakowski (2014) deploys Beck's theories to examine 'cosmopolitanism' in global football.
4 In fact, Horne and Jary (2004: 129) write that Giddens actually held an early academic interest in sport; his Masters dissertation explored sport and society in contemporary England.
5 Indeed, as Jarvis (2007: 45–46) suggests, rather than reading Beck in a purely empirical way, his ideas 'are perhaps better understood as a cultural and social commentary about the condition of late modernity and of its contradictions that both embody progress but also harm and risk'.

References

Albrow, M. (1996) *The Global Age*, Cambridge: Polity Press.

Aradau, C. and Van Munster, R. (2007) 'Governing Terrorism through Risk: Taking Precautions, (Un)knowing the Future', *European Journal of International Relations* 13(1): 89–115.

Aradau, C., Lobo-Guerrero, L. and Van Muster, R. (2008) 'Security, Technologies of Risk, and the Political: Guest Editors' Introduction', *Security Dialogue* 39(2–3): 147–154.

Armstrong, G. and Mitchell, J.P. (2008) *Global and Local Football: Politics and Europeanization on the Fringes of the EU*, London/New York: Routledge.

Bairner, A. (2001) *Sport, Nationalism, and Globalization: European and North American Perspectives*, New York: State University of New York Press.

Beck, U. (1987) 'The Anthropological Shock: Chernobyl and the Contours of the Risk Society', *Berkeley Journal of Sociology* 32: 153–165.

Beck, U. (1992) *Risk Society: Towards a New Modernity*, London: Sage.

Beck, U. (1999) *World Risk Society*, Cambridge: Polity Press.

Beck, U. (2000) *What is Globalization?*, Cambridge: Polity Press.

Beck, U. (2002) 'The Terrorist Threat: World Risk Society Revisited', *Theory, Culture & Society* 19(4): 39–55.

Beck, U. (2006) 'Living in the World Risk Society: A Hobhouse Memorial Public Lecture Given on Wednesday 15 February 2006 at the London School of Economics', *Economy and Society* 35(3): 329–345.

Beck, U. (2009) *World at Risk*, Cambridge: Polity Press.

Beck, U. (2016) *The Metamorphosis of the World*, Cambridge/Malden, MA: Polity.

Beck, U., Giddens, A. and Lash, S. (1994) *Reflexive Modernization: Politics, Tradition and Aesthetics in the Modern Social Order*, Oxford: Polity Press.

Burgess, A., Wardman, J. and Mythen, G. (2018) 'Considering Risk: Placing the Work of Ulrich Beck in Context', *Journal of Risk Research* 21(1): 1–5.

Castells, M. (2000) *The Rise of the Network Society*, Oxford: Blackwell.

Cleland, J. (2015) *A Sociology of Football in a Global Context*, London: Routledge.

Curran D. (2016) *Risk, Power, and Inequality in the 21st Century*, London: Palgrave Macmillan

David, M. and Millward, P. (2012) 'Football's Coming Home?: Digital Reterritorialization, Contradictions in the Transnational Coverage of Sport and the Sociology of Alternative Football Broadcasts', *The British Journal of Sociology* 63(2):349–369.

Dean, M. (1999) *Governmentality: Power and Rule in Modern Society*, London: Sage.

Dean, M. (2010) 'Power at the Heart of the Present: Exception, Risk and Sovereignty', *European Journal of Cultural Studies* 13(4): 459–475.

Doidge, M. (2015) *Football Italia: Italian Football in an Age of Globalization*, London: Bloomsbury.

Duke, V. (2002) 'Local Tradition Versus Globalisation: Resistance to the McDonaldisation and Disneyisation of Professional Football in England', *Football Studies* 5(1): 5–23.

Ekberg, M. (2007) 'The Parameters of the Risk Society: A Review and Exploration', *Current Sociology* 55(3): 343–366.

Ericson, R. and Haggerty, K. (1997) *Policing the Risk Society*, Toronto: University of Toronto Press.

Foer, F. (2005) *How Football Explains the World*, London: Arrow Books.

Flynn, R. (2002) 'Clinical Governance and Governmentality', *Health, Risk & Society* 4(2): 155–173.

Foucault, M. (1991[1978]) 'Governmentality', *The Foucault Effect* (Eds. G. Burchill, C. Gordon and P. Miller), London: Harvester Wheatsheaf, pp. 87–104.

Giddens, A. (1990) *The Consequences of Modernity*, Cambridge: Polity.

Giddens, A. (1999a) 'Risk and Responsibility', *The Modern Law Review* 62(1): 1–35.

Giddens, A. (1999b) 'Lecture 2 – Risk – Hong Kong', *BBC*, available from: http://news.bbc.co.uk/hi/english/static/events/reith_99/week2/week2.htm [Accessed 11/2021].

Giulianotti, R. (1999) *Football: A Sociology of the Global Game*, Cambridge: Polity.

Giulianotti, R. (2009) 'Risk and Sport: An Analysis of Sociological Theories and Research Agendas', *Sociology of Sport Journal* 26(4): 540–556.

Giulianotti, R. (2016) *Sport: A Critical Sociology*, Cambridge: Polity.

Giulianotti, R. and Robertson, R. (2004) 'The Globalization of Football: A Study in the Glocalization of the 'Serious Life', *The British Journal of Sociology* 55(4): 545–568.

Giulianotti, R. and Robertson, R. (2007) 'Recovering the Social: Globalization, Football and Transnationalism', *Global Networks* 7(2): 166–186.

Giulianotti, R. and Robertson, R. (2009) *Globalization and Football*, London: Sage.

Hanlon, G. (2010) 'Knowledge, Risk and Beck: Misconceptions of Expertise and Risk', *Critical Perspectives on Accounting* 21(3): 211–220.

Heng, Y.K. (2006) 'The "Transformation of War" Debate: Through the Looking Glass of Ulrich Beck's World Risk Society', *International Relations* 20(1): 69–91.

Hognestad, H. (2009) 'Transglobal Scandinavian? Globalization and the Contestation of Identities in Football', *Soccer & Society* 10(3–4): 358–373.

Horne, J. and Jary, D. (2004) 'Anthony Giddens: Structuration Theory, Sport and Leisure', *Sport and Modern Social Theorists* (Eds. R. Giulianotti), London: Palgrave, pp. 129–144.

Houlihan, B. and Giulianotti, R. (2012) 'Politics and the London 2012 Olympics: The (In)Security Games', *International Affairs* 88: 701–717.

Jarvis, D.S. (2007) 'Risk, Globalisation and The State: A Critical Appraisal of Ulrich Beck and the World Risk Society Thesis', *Global Society* 21(1): 23–46.

Jennings, W. (2012) *Olympic Risks*, Basingstoke: Palgrave.

Kelly, P. (2003) 'Growing Up as Risky Business? Risks, Surveillance and the Institutionalized Mistrust of Youth', *Journal of Youth Studies* 6(2): 165–180.

Kossakowski, R. (2014) 'The Cosmopolitan Game? Contemporary Football in the Light of Ulrich Beck's Theory', *Kultura I Edukacja* 5(105): 36–62.

Lee Ludvigsen, J.A. (2020) 'The Premier League-Globalization Nexus: Notes on Current Trends, Pressing Issues and Inter-Linked "-Ization" Processes', *Managing Sport and Leisure* 25(1–2): 37–51.

Lee Ludvigsen, J.A. and Millward, P. (2019) 'Global Elites and Sports Ownership: Emerging Economies "Foreign" Owners and New Strategies', *The Business and Culture of Sport* (Eds. J. Maguire, M. Falcous and K. Liston), Farmington Hills: Macmillan, pp. 167–180.

Lim, W.K. (2011) 'Understanding Risk Governance: Introducing Sociological Neoinstitutionalism and Foucauldian Governmentality for Further Theorizing', *International Journal of Disaster Risk Science* 2(3): 11–20.

Lupton, D. (1999) *Risk*, London: Routledge.

Millward, P. (2011) *The Global Football League: Transnational Networks, Social Movements and Sport in the New Media Age*, Basingstoke: Palgrave.

Mythen, G. (2004) *Ulrich Beck: A Critical Introduction to the Risk Society*, London: Pluto Press.

Mythen, G. (2005) 'Employment, Individualization and Insecurity: Rethinking the Risk Society Perspective', *The Sociological Review* 53(1): 129–149.

Mythen, G. (2018) 'Thinking with Ulrich Beck: Security, Terrorism and Transformation', *Journal of Risk Research* 21(1): 17–28.

Mythen, G. and Walklate, S. (2006) 'Criminology and Terrorism: Which Thesis? Risk Society Or Governmentality?', *British Journal of Criminology* 46(3): 379–398.

Mythen, G. and Walklate, S. (2008) 'Terrorism, Risk and International Security: The Perils of Asking "What If?"', *Security Dialogue* 39: 221–241.

Mythen, G. and Walklate, S. (2016) 'Not Knowing, Emancipatory Cata-strophism and Metamorphosis: Embracing the Spirit of Ulrich Beck', *Security Dialogue* 47(5): 403–419.

Nash, R. (2000) 'Globalised Football Fandom: Scandinavian Liverpool FC Supporters', *Football Studies* 3(2): 5–23.

Petersen-Wagner, R. (2017) 'The Football Supporter in a Cosmopolitan Epoch', *Journal of Sport and Social Issues* 41(2): 133–150.

Petersen-Wagner, R. (2019) 'Between Old and New Traditions: Transnational Solidarities and the Love for Liverpool FC', *Digital Football Cultures* (Eds. S. Lawrence and G. Crawford), Abingdon: Routledge, 47–66.

Robertson, R. (1992) *Globalization: Social Theory and Global Culture*, London: Sage.

Robertson, R. and White, K.E. (2007) 'What is Globalisation?', *The Blackwell Companion to Globalisation* (Eds. G. Ritzer), Malden: Blackwell Publishing, pp. 54–66.

Sandvoss, C. (2003) *A Game of Two Halves: Football, Television and Globalization*, London: Routledge.

Zinn, J.O. and Taylor-Gooby, P. (2006) 'Risk as an Interdisciplinary Research Area', *Risk in Social Science* (Eds. P. Taylor-Gooby and J.O. Zinn), Oxford: Oxford University Press, pp. 20–53.

Wardman, J.K. and Lofstedt, R. (2020) 'COVID-19: Confronting a New World Risk', *Journal of Risk Research* 23(7–8): 833–837.

3 Between Environmental and Political Risks

The World Cup, 'Green Legacies' and Protests

Introduction

Between 31 October and 13 November 2021, the 26th United Nations (UN) Climate Change Conference – more commonly known as COP26 – was held in Glasgow, Scotland. One of the conference's key aims, as attended by hundreds of state leaders, politicians, scientists and innovators, related to the mitigation of climate change. In the context of individuals' and institutions' enhanced reflexivity which characterizes the modern era, sustainability and responding to environmental risks feature centrally on the political and societal agendas of the present-day (Beck, 2010, 2016). Indeed, the adaption of low-carbon social and economic models is integral in order to meet the goal of the 2015 Paris Agreement of keeping global warming below 2°C (Müller et al., 2021), whilst the centrality of the environment and climate change has generated a turn towards 'greening initiatives' and climate-friendly policies amongst governments, institutions and societies (Death, 2011).

Increasingly, however, sport mega-events such as the *Fédération Internationale de Football Association* (FIFA) World Cup and the Olympic Games have joined in on this trend. Presently, environmental impact assessments represent a significant aspect of World Cup bids, requirements and their envisaged legacies (Death, 2011; Horne, 2014; Ross and Orr, 2022). Further, during COP26, FIFA also pledged their commitment to the UN's new climate targets including net-zero emission by 2040 and a 50% reduction in greenhouse gases by 2030 (BBC Sport, 2021). Coinciding with COP26, FIFA (2021) also published their new 'FIFA Climate Strategy' aiming to make the organization and its tournaments more climate-friendly.

This chapter employs the football World Cup as a case to explore the inter-connecting environmental and political risks that emerge – and

DOI: 10.4324/9781003303480-3

are *responded to* – in the most popular football competition globally. Every World Cup is surrounded by risks and uncertainty. Not only may World Cups be threatened by the environmental hazards of heavy rain or extreme heat (Ross and Orr, 2022), but all sport mega-events in the twenty-first century carry significant carbon costs and have material environmental impacts (Horne, 2014). These include, *inter alia*, the production of waste, consumption of energy, urban developments and stadium constructions, transport and international and domestic travelling (ibid.). Critically, as this chapter shows, some of these issues can – for (prospective) host nations – translate into distinct political risks speaking to public opposition against World Cup-related stadium constructions, so-called 'white elephants' and 'legacies'. Particularly in an age where the financial, social and environmental costs of sport mega-events like the World Cup have been criticized and increasingly protested against by campaigners, activists and local residents of host cities (Cornelissen, 2012; Zirin, 2016).

Drawing from publicly available bidding documents (related to the 2026 World Cup), press releases and the published literature, this chapter begins with a socio-historical contextualization of the World Cup, its legacy discourses and continual expansions. I also zoom in on the forthcoming 2026 World Cup that, for the first time, will involve 48 qualified teams and be co-hosted by three countries: Canada, Mexico and the USA (Beissel and Kohe, 2020). Then, the chapter discusses the World Cup's 'greening' programs and initiatives (cf. Death, 2011) as a continual reflexive trend also identifiable within the successful 2026 bid. Finally, the chapter takes a step back to examine some of the inter-connected political risks that may emerge as the staging of the World Cup increasingly impact host countries' social *and* natural environments. For some countries, the staging of World Cups, as vividly demonstrated by previous examples, can lead to political backlashes speaking to 'anti-mega-event' sentiment, protests and campaigning on a civil society level.

Socio-historical context: the World Cup, its expansion and the 'United bid'

Staged in four-year cycles, the men's World Cup, administered by football's governing body FIFA, is one of *the* biggest sport mega-events along with the Olympics. The truly global football tournament is visited by enormous numbers of fans and tourists and broadcast in over 200 national territories (Horne, 2014). In line with elite football's intensified commodifying processes (Giulianotti, 2002), so has the cost for the event's commercial and broadcasting rights ballooned. Illustrating this, the sale of the tournament's broadcasting rights for the 2018 and 2022 editions reportedly generated £1.15 billion for FIFA (The Guardian, 2011). Ultimately, FIFA and World Cup have been subjected to substantial academic research. This includes academic work on topics like the World Cup's political economy (Horne and Manzenreiter, 2006), corruption (Sugden and Tomlinson, 2017), security (Eisenhauer et al., 2014) and the World Cup's social, urban or economic 'impacts' or 'legacies' (Alm et al., 2016; Horne and Manzenreiter, 2004; Millward, 2017, Millward et al., in press).

Since its foundation in 1930, the World Cup has continually expanded in terms of qualified teams,[1] commercial activities and partnerships, and the organizational demands and costs for selected host nations (Tomlinson, 2000).[2] Yet, as Horne (2014: 12) writes, this has also been paralleled by the expansion of World Cup 'legacy discourses' that have 'become a necessary corollary to the enormous staging costs, which could not be justified by local organizers or politicians for a four-week spectacular alone'. As a broad and contested mega-event phenomenon, legacy discourses have mushroomed in a time characterized by an increased political and public awareness and scrutiny of the possible negative side-effects of sport mega-events, their financial costs, infrastructure constructions and impacts on the environment. However, as noted:

> Like a lot of contemporary corporate-speak legacy is a term that incorporates an orientation to the future and implies there will be no turning back ('going forward') whilst at the same time it can be used by promoters to play a part in 'winning consent' from potentially sceptical local populations to developments that are not automatically socially, economically or environmentally acceptable.
>
> (Horne, 2014: 12)

Furthermore, as the organizational, infrastructural and financial demands that World Cup host countries sign up to have grown apace, some countries have turned towards co-hosting events or the setup of bidding alliances (Horne and Manzenreiter, 2004; Wise and Lee Ludvigsen, 2022). Here, the upcoming 2026 World Cup stands out as unprecedented. Canada, Mexico and the USA's highly politicized 2026 World Cup bid was successful on 13 June 2018. The bid, known as the 'United bid', beat Morocco's rivalling bid by a final vote of 134 to 65 (Beissel and Kohe, 2020). However, this World Cup edition will not solely be the first one to be staged across *three* host countries (Lee

Ludvigsen, 2019).[3] It will also be the first World Cup boasting a 48-team format following FIFA's (2017) decision to expand from 32 to 48 qualified teams for the 2026 World Cup finals. Overall, this means that the 2026 World Cup will involve 80 games (Beissel and Kohe, 2020) that will take place across 16 stadiums (2 in Canada, 3 in Mexico and 11 in the USA).

As this pioneering World Cup case has approached in time, it has been subject to growing academic interest (see Beissel and Kohe, 2020; Lee Ludvigsen, 2019; Ross and Orr, 2022; Wise and Ludvigsen, 2022). Although every World Cup version possesses unique risk profiles (see Wong and Chadwick, 2017), the 2026 edition arguably gives insights into some of the most pressing risks and trends *vis-à-vis* global football, legacies and the environment. This includes the so-called 'greening' of World Cups and their legacies (cf. Death, 2011).

'Greening' initiatives, strategies and legacies

As a basic starting point, Miller (2016: 719) reminds us that global mega-events like the World Cup are both 'directly and indirectly environmentally destructive' since they involve, among other things, the maintenance of football grounds with the use of chemicals and water, electricity that powers stadiums and the enormous impact of travelling related to World Cup tourism and transport. In their delineation of the aforementioned 'millennial phase' of football's globalization, Giulianotti and Robertson (2009: 39) asserted that: 'We may anticipate future concerns over the "carbon footprints" that are imprinted by the global movement of peoples when attending these major championships'. In many ways, such anticipation has proved accurate, and scholars are now increasingly examining the relationship between sport mega-events and their environmental impacts and ('greening') initiatives or legacies (Boykoff, 2021; Karamichas, 2013; Miller, 2018; Preuss, 2013; Ross and Orr, 2022; Samuel and Stubbs, 2013).

In the wider sports world, Boykoff and Mascarenhas (2016) point towards the UN's 1992 Earth Summit and the subsequent publication of the 'Agenda 21' action plan. Following these landmark events, they note that the International Olympic Committee (IOC) started to place a heavier emphasis on concerns for environmental issues in their Olympic Charter (see also Karamichas, 2013: 100–101). Currently, similar practices may be identified across several other sports federations. Whereas the literature on the World Cup, its 'green' legacies and economies remains under-developed, several environmental initiatives can be identified before, during and after World Cups (Preuss,

2013; Ross and Orr, 2022). While this demonstrates a more pronounced organizational awareness regarding the World Cup's environmental impacts and environmental issues more widely, some researchers argue that this strategy or trend could also be read as 'corporate environmentalism' (Lenskyj, 1998), 'event greening' (Death, 2011) or even 'greenwashing' (Miller, 2018).

According to Death (2011), 'event greening' has two key dimensions built into it. First, that is the mitigation of the 'direct environmental impact of "footprint" of the event' (p. 101). Second, the potential of sporting events to act as catalysts for socio-political 'legacies' speaking to sustainability. One such example is the 'Green Goal programme' associated with Germany's 2006 World Cup. The target of this initiative was to reduce the World Cup's impact on the global climate to the minimum (FIFA, 2005) with a programme that addressed water, waste, energy, transportation and carbon offsetting which, at its time, aimed to make the 2006 tournament the 'greenest' tournament thus far (Ross and Orr, 2022). Following this, FIFA has continually encouraged local organizing committees to address environmental protection in their hosting rights bids (Horne, 2014). Accordingly, a 'Green Goal 2010' programme was developed for South Africa's 2010 World Cup. Inspired by the 2006 World Cup, this initiative 'sought to create a positive legacy from the tournament across the three pillars of sustainable development: social, economic and environmental' (Death, 2011: 100). Though, despite this, Death notes that the World Cup, still ended up being the most 'carbon-intensive' World Cup ever, at its time (p. 108).

What remains most central in this chapter's discussion, however, is the 'marked increase in environmental planning and awareness' around the World Cup (Ross and Orr, 2022: 871) which in itself implies an attempt to pre-emptively mitigate environmental *risks*. In a way, following Beck's (1992: 37) lead, this demonstrates risks' reactionary 'boomerang effect', which means that even the society's wealthiest and most powerful organizations cannot escape the risks they contribute towards, which 'catch up with those who produce or profit from [risk]'.

As stated, FIFA (2021) recently confirmed their commitment to the COP26 initiatives. The organization launched a 20-page long document centred around four key pillars: education, adaption, investment and reduction. Further, before the forthcoming 2026 World Cup, several 'greening' initiatives and discourses can be found in the relevant bidding documents, showing how environmental issues feature centrally in the event planning and legacy phases. This includes a 97-page long 'Environmental Impact Assessment' of the bid, which not only refers to the term 'sustainability' on 96 occasions, but highlights that the bid's aim is to accelerate positive changes throughout the host cities and that the 2026 event presents a:

> unique opportunity not just to avoid exacerbating existing environmental conditions, but to be a force for good, catalyzing positive environmental change through the tournament stage and into legacy.
>
> (United as One, 2018: 2)

The 'Environmental Impact Assessment' also attests that 'Environmental sustainability is integral to [the bid's] entire approach and is not an "extra" or "nice to have"' and it cites specific mitigation and enhancement measures in the host cities speaking to *inter alia* carbon and climate change, energy, transport, air quality and waste management (ibid.: 3). In addition to the bid's framing of environmental 'legacies', the executive summary of the successful bid states that the tournament will be the 'greenest' World Cup of the modern era (United 2026, 2018: 11) and refers to the bid's 'Sustainability+' approach designed specifically to 'go beyond the requirements outlined by FIFA, to contribute measurably to sustainable development in our three countries, and to share what we've learned with the rest of the world' (ibid.: 16).

While such initiatives appear welcome at face value, they must also be approached with some caution. Historically, mega-events' pre-event legacy discourses and the eventual realities do not necessarily nor always match each other (Boykoff, 2020). Further, for Boykoff (2016: 147) the term 'sustainability', when applied to sport, is 'a notoriously slushy term, a big-business buzzword. All too often, sustainability rhetoric is a prettified scrim obscuring capitalism's incessant rapacity'. In a way, the legacy discourses could reinforce Beck's (2016: 45) observation that '"sustainability" [nowadays] has become normalized; everything is now about greening'. Further, some would perhaps point toward a contradiction: sport's governing bodies have increased the volume and frequency of its environmental and decarbonization discourses and requirements whilst concurrently increasing the relevant events' sizes and impacts (Boykoff and Gaffney, 2020; Horne, 2014). Hence, whilst there is an increased set of requirements imposed on host countries and cities to sufficiently address environmental sustainability (Ross and Orr, 2022), the World Cup has also expanded from 32 to 48 teams and in terms of geographic distances/footprints before 2026. Indeed, one projection suggests that the shift towards 48 teams is likely to significantly increase the tournament's fan travels, carbon footprints and hotel demands (see Pereira et al., 2020). Additionally, as Chapter 6 discusses, FIFA has also recently proposed the idea of a bi-annual rather than quadrennial World Cup (BBC Sport, 2021) whilst some of its current sponsors are high-carbon airline and motoring companies.[4] In spite of such contradictions, a continuation of the 'greening' initiatives (cf. Death, 2011; Miller, 2018) may nonetheless be observed in the 2020s.

Yet, there is another important aspect of the 'greening' of World Cups and their legacies. As I argue, this demonstrates an embedded organizational reflexivity *vis-à-vis* environmental risks and a 'pending global emergency' (Beck, 2016: 37) in the domain of global football. More broadly, this echoes the (risk) societies in which social concerns about climate change and taking precautionary measures to mitigate the risks from it (Domingues, 2021) are characterizing features influencing organizations and social institutions alike.

Political risks: 'white elephants', protests and backlash

The housing of a World Cup impacts both natural and social environments and, as discussed now, these impacts may prove contentious. This section unpacks some of the political and economic risks associated with the World Cup with reference to post-event under-utilization of World Cup stadiums, the (lack of) legacies and protests related to the World Cup's financial, social and environmental impacts. As a backdrop here, it is necessary to highlight that nations historically have hosted, and presently host World Cups for the tournament's supposed political-economic benefits and potential rewards. These may speak to nation-branding, tourism, urban legacies or the (re)ignition of a national identity (Rookwood, 2019). As I argue, countries' quest for such event-related benefits or rewards ultimately composes a risk and has distinct costs, whereas the 'prospective political returns from such "mega" events and projects must be offset against their high level of risk and complexity, invariably controversial or divisive politics, and poor track records in terms of cost overruns' (Jennings, 2013: 3). As Street et al. explain:

> The hosting of mega-sport events and all the associated activities that take place before, during and after can cause damage to the local physical environment. This could occur through the development and operations of expensive facilities and venues, the use of non-renewable resources and building materials.
>
> (Street et al., 2014: 121)

The staging of World Cups comes at astronomical financial costs for host countries. Often, this means that public resources are invested into infrastructures and hypermodern football stadiums where fixtures will take place (Gaffney, 2016). Importantly, however, the construction of expensive football stadiums does not always nor necessarily 'correspond with popular demand' (Horne and Manzenreiter, 2004: 190). Whereas the stadiums for the 2026 World Cup, predominantly, will be pre-existing and already in use (Lee Ludvigsen, 2019) the recent history of the World Cup powerfully illustrates that several stadium constructions and developments built specifically for host nations' World Cups have turned into what is oft-characterized in the literature as 'white-elephants' (Alm et al., 2016; Davis, 2019).

In a nutshell, 'white-elephants' refer to state-of-the-art stadiums that are specifically constructed for temporally limited events (e.g., the Olympics or World Cup) but where the stadiums' practical post-event value remains limited (Davis, 2019; Lee Ludvigsen, 2021) and where host nations have failed to maintain the stadium's standards, or 'found it difficult to fill up stadiums after the circuses have left town' (Alm et al., 2016: 564). At first glance, this appears strikingly incompatible with the regular pre-event political rhetoric, which typically justifies the use of public resources on stadiums by optimistically pointing towards the potential positive 'legacies' or 'impacts' the stadiums may have after an event. Indeed, bidding committees and governments commonly emphasize that tournament's civic and national legacies will 'remain long after these brief sporting extravaganzas have left town' (Giulianotti and Klauser, 2010: 53). However, to reiterate, in the universe of giant socio-urban projects like the World Cup or the Olympic Games, 'legacies' do not always materialize as promised or estimated in pre-event predictions (Boykoff, 2020). Therefore, one political risk is the over-promising of mega-events' benefits and their positive effects (Müller, 2015), which increasingly are critically questioned, resisted or even protested against by sub-political actors or members of the public.

By rewinding the recent social history of the World Cup, there are some striking examples of 'white elephants'. Before the 2002 World Cup which Japan co-hosted with South Korea, the former reportedly spent more than US$4 billion on ten new stadiums whose capacity massively exceeded the actual demand in the Japanese J-League (Horne and Manzenreiter, 2004). In the cases of the *Miyagi Stadium* and *Ecopa Stadium*, local football clubs even opted to play their games at other stadiums that were 'more suitable' and 'more adaptable' to their average attendance (Alm et al., 2016). Not too dissimilarly, similar issues emerged after the 2010 World Cup in South Africa where several of the stadiums constructed for the month-long tournament experienced post-event utilization problems, whilst FIFA's stadium requirements exceeded the local needs (ibid.).

More recently for Brazil's 2014 World Cup, Zirin (2016) writes that the requirement of providing 'FIFA-quality stadiums' did not merely prove economically costly, but also had large impacts on the local environment in the Amazon rainforest:

> The World Cup – which was a national operation, as opposed to the Rio-centric [2016] Olympics – meant greater stress on this critical ecosystem [the Amazon]. This was seen most sharply in the construction of a "FIFA-quality stadium" in Manaus, located in the middle of the Amazon rainforest. Brazil spent three hundred million dollars, almost fifteen million more than the original estimates, while uprooting acres of the most ecologically delicate region on the planet.
>
> (Zirin, 2016: 45)

Notwithstanding, as a post-event journalistic investigation by *The New York Times* (2016) suggested, two years after the 44,000-seater *Arena da Amazônia* had staged four fixtures during Brazil's World Cup, the arena had been left largely abandoned and was perceived by some local residents to represent a 'white elephant' that proved little practical use beyond the occasional visit from tourists. In this chapter's context, this remains relevant because the requirements imposed on the host countries and cities staging a World Cup – and the consequent public expenditure – constitute a significant political risk for governments, authorities and local organizing committees pursuing (and possibly securing) an event's hosting rights. They also enormously impact local residents and natural environments.

In the present-day, there is a marked public opposition and resistance to neoliberal sports mega-events like the Olympics (Boykoff, 2020, 2021; Giulianotti et al., 2015) and the World Cup (Cornelissen, 2012; Zirin, 2016). Increasingly, campaign groups and social movements call into question FIFA's demands and the World Cup's economic, social and environmental impacts. In sporting contexts, environmental protests may for example be staged against event-related installations on public land, the redevelopment of green spaces (Giulianotti et al., 2015) or high-carbon event sponsors. Moreover, Boykoff (2020) recently observed how anti-Olympic activists have become increasingly transnational in their campaigns to stop the Olympic Games from taking place.

Such glocalized activism-related trends may also be identified in the World Cup's context. The World Cup provides a specific moment around which more deep-lying issues, *inter alia*, public spending, militarization, securitization, human rights and environmental (in)justice can be resisted. As Cornelissen (2012) points out, the World Cup has increasingly become a nucleus of social activism and 'anti-mega-event' campaigning which opposes local and global trends encapsulated by the gigantic football tournament. Cornelissen writes that:

> In the current era, new generations of social movements concerning themselves with the ethics of neoliberal globalization have taken on board the issue of mega-events, thus enabling both the transnationalization of 'local' (domestic) issues and the localization of transnational dynamics.
>
> (ibid.: 334)

In South Africa, the enormous costs of hosting the 2010 World Cup were one of the key issues that were protested. Demonstrations taking place highlighted concerns related to the World Cup and its infrastructural and policy changes which diverted money and resources away from more pressing social priorities like housing. Indeed, between 2007 and 2010, over 70,000 workers participated in strikes related to World Cup projects (Zirin, 2016) thereby delaying the progress on and completion of the stadium and infrastructure construction before the competition (Wong and Chadwick, 2017). Then, in relation to the 'Green Goal's' claims of environmental sustainability, Death (2011: 108) argues that social movement activists saw this as 'laughable' and a case of 'greenwashing'. However, protests have not been confined to this tournament. In Brazil, large-scale protests emerged before Brazil's 2013 Confederations Cup (Gaffney, 2016)[5] and the 2014 World Cup (Zirin, 2016). This included protestors with banners reading 'FIFA Go Home', who marched through Rio de Janeiro ahead of the 2014 World Cup's opening ceremony (The Guardian, 2014). Whilst the protests in certain ways were centred on the World Cup and its related social, environmental and financial costs, they also reflected the deeper and more long-standing domestic issues speaking to forced removals, education, hospitals and police brutality (The Guardian, 2014; Zirin, 2016). One of the key grievances, however, included the 'misuse of public money on unsustainable construction projects' specifically for the World Cup (Miller, 2016: 724).

Taken together, and accepting the above examples' diverse geographies, social contexts and political systems, all this remains significant given how accurately it encapsulates how there are some serious political risks and backlashes associated with countries' strategic pursuit of and staging of World Cups. Countries and cities may envisage, or consciously aspire to employ sporting spectacles for political gains or benefits speaking to the accumulation of 'soft power' (Rookwood, 2019), the creation of national identities, a nationwide 'feel-good' effect (Cornelissen and Maennig, 2010) or a 'social euphoria' (Boykoff, 2014). Notwithstanding, the issues of unsustainable costs and FIFA's demands – coupled with deeper local struggles – are increasingly protested on a civil society level by sub-political actors and can mobilize public opposition and a 'anti-mega-event' sentiment, as the examples powerfully illustrate (Cornelissen, 2012).

New era, new challenges?

Altogether, the editions of FIFA's flagship tournament represent moments for local residents, campaigners and social movements to express their long-standing *and* event-specific dissent. As shown, some of the expressed concerns relate to the use of public resources on new stadiums that may damage and/or negatively influence the local environments (Street et al., 2014). Faced with prospects of public backlash, Lauermann (2022: 5) suggests that some city leaders and sport mega-event promoters now look increasingly towards socio-urban projects that are 'less politically risky' than mega-events. Indeed, Müller et al. (2021) recently suggested that sport mega-events have now reached their 'peak event' and that their sizes and impacts will begin to decline following a period of crisis. They argue that the transition into a 'digital, carbon-constrained and pandemic-aware world – will require mega-events to reinvent themselves' (ibid.: 27). Hence, in the forthcoming case of the 2026 World Cup – with its relative absence of new stadia – it remains particularly interesting to observe how issues associated with other costs and the excessive travelling induced by the three-host format may create backlashes from social movements and environmental groups.

However, already in July 2021, Montreal withdrew its candidacy as a 2026 host city over cost concerns. As reported, this followed an increase in the estimated costs from $50 to $103 million and Quebec's Tourism Minister Caroline Proulx had earlier said that: 'In the current context, we consider that the priority remains to support Quebecers and businesses in times of pandemic and towards economic recovery' (quoted in CTV News, 2021). Further, the pre-event phase of the 2026 World Cup has already seen social movements voice their concerns. In late November 2021, while the final host cities were being finalized, 'Unite Here Local 11' – a labour union representing over 32,000 tourism workers in the Los Angeles region – rallied during an official FIFA venue visit at Rose Bowl stadium in Pasadena, California. Fronting a large banner stating 'FIFA Workers Rights are Human Rights',[6] the rally sought to draw attention to the selection of equitable and fair stadiums for the 2026 World Cup and the protection of human and workers' rights (Yahoo News, 2021). This goes some way to reinforce what scholar and activist Simon Black (2018) argues; that the 'Pan-American' tournament represents a moment to oppose the World Cup's controversial sides and political double standards:

> So what are players and fans, activists and socialists to do? The beautiful game is not irredeemably tainted, but its greatest competition certainly is. While the player and fan in me welcomes the World Cup to Canada, the activist and socialist in me knows that 2026 is an opportunity to agitate, educate, and organize.
>
> (Black, 2018)

Additionally, the recent, contentious and commercially driven proposal (or reinvention, see Müller et al. 2021) from FIFA to stage the World Cup bi-annually – rather than quadrennially (see Chapter 6) – is likely to impact, in distinct ways, public opinion on the World Cup and its housing in the 2020s. In all, the World Cup's footprint, political economy, and increasingly centrifugal impacts on social, urban and natural environments mean that the competition is not solely a catalyst for many governments, but for civic activism too.

Conclusion: with football comes great risks?

This chapter argues that precautionary principles and publicly expressed social concerns *vis-à-vis* environmental risks have become increasingly embedded into the biggest football mega-event globally. In an age where environmental risk and its governance feature centrally on the political and public agendas (Beck, 2016), such an argument is substantial in magnitude since it yields an insight into one domain of the global politics of the environment. Each World Cup is surrounded by environmental and political uncertainties. Environmental risks like heavy rain, extreme heat or typhoons are not merely risks that are faced by the World Cup's organizers and stakeholders, as risk that may jeopardize event fixtures and athletes' and spectators' safety. It is also a type of risk that the staging of a World Cup can exacerbate (Ross and Orr, 2022) through the production of waste, urban development, excessive air travels and event-related stadium constructions (Horne, 2014; Miller, 2016; Millward et al., in press). As this chapter argues, the environmental risks and damages and wider socio-economic impacts of World Cups may also be inter-connected with or translate into a set of political risks – or 'political banana skins' (Jennings, 2013: 3) such as an elevated 'anti-mega-event' sentiment taking shape as public opposition and protest (Cornelissen, 2012). Essentially, it can be claimed that both locally and globally '[p]olitics constitutes another area of risk in football' (Kossakowski, 2014: 55).

In the present-day, as discussed above, one may observe 'greening' discourses, rhetoric and legacies surrounding sport mega-events (Death, 2011; Samuel and Stubbs, 2013). Increasingly, specific initiatives and precautionary principles have been generated by sport's governing bodies who set out standards and requirements that address environmental issues and climate change. Accordingly, World Cup bids increasingly devote a space to environmental concerns and initiatives (Death, 2011). Despite this, Ross and Orr (2022: 882) argue that challenges remain speaking to the 'actual implementation of environmental initiatives and responsibility for their success post-event'. Indeed, this again ignites questions regarding which actors remain responsible for ensuring that 'climate-friendly' and environmental legacies materialize, and then, the consequences for potential mismatches between pre-event promises and post-event realities. As argued throughout this chapter, however, these tendencies and the 'climate politics' discourses (cf. Beck, 2010) can also be understood to encapsulate an enhanced institutional reflexivity which has been embedded 'into' the practices of the football World Cup, its governors and football federations and is publicly expressed. This reflexivity relates to the more widespread social concerns of the potentially catastrophic effect of environmental risks (Beck, 1992), and the need to (publicly) address these which – after all – remains a key characteristic of global risk societies.

Notes

1 Illustrated by the expansion from 16 to 24 teams before the 1982 World Cup and from 24 to 32 teams before the 1998 World Cup (see Horne, 2014).
2 For example, Front Office Sport (2021) report that the total costs of Qatar's 2022 World Cup are in the region of $300 billion.

3   To date, the only World Cup hosted by more than one country is the 2002
    World Cup in South Korea and Japan.
4   See: https://www.reuters.com/article/us-sport-climate-idUKKBN2BF1W8
    (Accessed 12/2021).
5   The Confederations Cup is typically staged in the country that will be the
    World Cup host the following year.
6   See: https://twitter.com/unitehere11?lang=eu (Accessed 11/2021).

References

Alm, J., Solberg, H.A., Storm, R.K. and Jakobsen, T.G. (2016) 'Hosting Major
    Sports Events: The Challenge of Taming White Elephants', *Leisure Studies*
    35(5): 564–582.
BBC Sport (2021) 'COP26: FIFA Signs up to New UN Climate Targets for
    Sport Despite Proposing Biennial World Cup', available from: https://www.
    bbc.co.uk/sport/59150667.
Beck, U. (1992) *Risk Society: Towards a New Modernity*, London: Sage.
Beck, U. (2010) 'Climate for Change, or How to Create a Green Modernity?',
    Theory, Culture & Society 27(2–3): 254–266.
Beck, U. (2016) *The Metamorphosis of the World*, Cambridge/Malden, MA: Polity.
Beissel, A.S. and Kohe, G. (2020) 'United as One: The 2026 FIFA Men's
    World Cup Hosting Vision and the Symbolic Politics of Legacy', *Managing
    Sport and Leisure*: 1–21.
Black, S. (2018) 'The World Cup Is a Crime Scene', *Canadian Dimension*,
    available   from   https://canadiandimension.com/articles/view/the-world-
    cup-is-a-crime-scene [Accessed 11/2021].
Boykoff, J. (2014) *Celebration Capitalism and the Olympic Games*, London/New
    York: Routledge.
Boykoff, J. (2016) *Power Games: A Political History of the Olympics*,
    London/New York: Verso Books.
Boykoff, J. (2020) *Nolympians: Inside the Fight against Capitalist Mega-Sports
    in Los Angeles, Tokyo & Beyond*, Winnipeg: Fernwood.
Boykoff, J. (2021) 'Olympic Sustainability or Olympian Smokescreen', *Nature
    Sustainability* 4(4): 294–295.
Boykoff, J. and Gaffney, C. (2020) 'The Tokyo 2020 Games and the End of
    Olympic History', *Capitalism Nature Socialism* 31(2): 1–19.
Boykoff, J. and Mascarenhas, G. (2016) 'The Olympics, Sustainability, and
    Greenwashing: The Rio 2016 Summer Games', *Capitalism Nature Socialism*
    27(2): 1–11.
Cornelissen, S. and Maennig, W. (2010) 'On the Political Economy of "Feel-
    good" Effects at Sport Mega-Events: Experiences from FIFA Germany
    2006 and Prospects for South Africa 2010', *Alternation* 17(2): 96–120.
Cornelissen, S. (2012) '"Our Struggles Are Bigger Than the World Cup": Civic
    Activism, State-Society Relations and the Socio-Political Legacies of the
    2010 FIFA World Cup', *British Journal of Sociology* 63(2): 328–348.

CTV News (2021) 'Montreal Withdraws from 2026 FIFA World Cup Consideration', available from: https://montreal.ctvnews.ca/montreal-withdraws-from-2026-fifa-world-cup-consideration-1.5498242 [Accessed 11/2021].

Davis, J. (2019) 'Avoiding White Elephants? The Planning and Design of London's 2012 Olympic and Paralympic Venues, 2002–2018', *Planning Perspectives* 35(5), 827–848.

Death, C. (2011) '"Greening" the 2010 FIFA World Cup: Environmental Sustainability and the Mega-Event in South Africa', *Journal of Environmental Policy & Planning* 13(2): 99–117.

Domingues, J.M. (2021) 'Climate Change and Its Lexicon: An Analytical and Critical View', *International Journal of Politics, Culture, and Society*: 1–16.

Eisenhauer, S., Adair, D. and Taylor, T. (2014) 'Fifa-isation: Security, Brand Protection and Media Management at the 2010 World Cup in South Africa', *Surveillance & Society* 11(4): 377–391.

FIFA (2005) 'GREEN GOAL Internet Offering Launched', available from: https://www.fifa.com/tournaments/mens/worldcup/2006germany/-media-releases/green-goal-internet-offering-launched-25279 [Accessed 12/2021].

FIFA (2017) 'Unanimous Decision Expands FIFA World Cup™ to 48 Teams from 2026', available from: https://www.fifa.com/tournaments/mens/worldcup/canadamexicousa2026/media-releases/fifa-council-unanimously-decides-on-expansion-of-the-fifa-world-cuptm--2863100.

FIFA (2021) *FIFA Climate Strategy: Making Football Climate Resilient and Mitigating Our Impact on the Climate*: 1–20, available from: https://digitalhub.fifa.com/m/a6e93d3f1e33b09/original/FIFA-Climate-Strategy.pdf [Accessed 12/2021].

Front Office Sports (2021) 'Qatar Expects $20 Billion Economic Boost from World Cup', available from https://frontofficesports.com/world-cup-2022-to-bring-in-20b-for-qatar/.

Gaffney, C. (2016) 'An Anatomy of Resistance: The Popular Committees of the FIFA World Cup in Brazil', *Sport, Protest and Globalisation: Stopping Play* (Eds. J. Dart and S. Wagg), London: Palgrave Macmillan, pp. 335–364.

Giulianotti, R. (2002) 'Supporters, Followers, Fans, and Flaneurs: A Taxonomy of Spectator Identities in Football', *Journal of Sport and Social Issues* 26(1): 25–46.

Giulianotti, R. and Klauser, F. (2010) 'Security Governance and Sport Mega-Events: Toward an Interdisciplinary Research Agenda', *Journal of Sport and Social Issues* 34(1): 49–61.

Giulianotti, R. and Robertson, R. (2009) *Globalization and Football*, London: Sage.

Giulianotti, R., Armstrong, G., Hales, G. and Hobbs, D. (2015) 'Sport Mega-Events and Public Opposition: A Sociological Study of the London 2012 Olympics', *Journal of Sport and Social Issues* 39(2): 99–119.

Horne, J. (2014) 'Managing World Cup Legacy', *Managing the World Cup* (Eds. S. Frawley and D. Adair), London: Palgrave, pp. 7–25.

Horne, J.D. and Manzenreiter, W. (2004) 'Accounting for Mega-Events: Forecast and Actual Impacts of the 2002 Football World Cup Finals on the Host Countries Japan/Korea', *International Review for the Sociology of Sport* 39(2): 187–203.

Horne, J. and Manzenreiter, W. (2006) 'An Introduction to the Sociology of Sports Mega-Events', *The Sociological Review* 54(2): 1–24.

Jennings, W. (2013) 'Governing the Games: High Politics, Risk and Mega-Events', *Political Studies Review* 11(1): 2–14.

Karamichas, J. (2013) *The Olympic Games and the Environment*, Basingstoke: Palgrave Macmillan.

Kossakowski, R. (2014) 'The Cosmopolitan Game? Contemporary Football in the light of Ulrich Beck's Theory', *Kultura I Edukacja* 5(105): 36–62.

Lauermann, J. (2022) 'The Declining Appeal of Mega-Events in Entrepreneurial Cities: From Los Angeles 1984 to Los Angeles 2028', *EPC: Politics and Space* 1–16. https://doi.org/10.1177/23996544211066101

Lee Ludvigsen, J.A. (2019) '"Continent-wide" Sports Spectacles: The "Multiple Host Format" of Euro 2020 and United 2026 and Its Implications', *Journal of Convention & Event Tourism* 20(2): 163–181.

Lee Ludvigsen, J.A. (2021) 'Mega-Events, Expansion and Prospects: Perceptions of Euro 2020 and Its 12-Country Hosting Format', *Journal of Consumer Culture* 1–19. https://doi.org/10.1177/14695405211026045

Lenskyj, H.J. (1998) 'Sport and Corporate Environmentalism: The Case of the Sydney 2000 Olympics', *International Review for the Sociology of Sport* 33(4): 341–354.

Miller, T. (2016) 'Greenwashed Sports and Environmental Activism: Formula 1 and FIFA', *Environmental Communication* 10(6): 719–733.

Miller, T. (2018) *Greenwashing Sport*, London: Routledge.

Millward, P. (2017) 'World Cup 2022 and Qatar's Construction Projects: Relational Power in Networks and Relational Responsibilities to Migrant Workers', *Current Sociology* 65(5): 756–776.

Millward, P., Lee Ludvigsen, J.A. and Sly, J. (in press) *Sport and Crime: Towards a Critical Criminology of Sport*, Routledge.

Müller, M. (2015) 'The Mega-Event Syndrome: Why So Much Goes Wrong in Mega-Event Planning and What To Do about It', *Journal of the American Planning Association* 81(1): 6–17.

Müller, M., Gogishvili, D., Wolfe, S.D., Gaffney, C., Hug, M. and Leick, A. (2021) 'Peak Event: The Rise, Crisis and Decline of Large Events (June 21, 2021)', available at SSRN: https://ssrn.com/abstract=3873972.

Pereira, R.P.T., Filimonau, V. and Ribeiro, G.M. (2020) 'Projecting the Carbon Footprint of Tourist Accommodation at the 2030 FIFA World Cup^{TM}', *Cleaner and Responsible Consumption* 1: 1–10.

Preuss, H. (2013) 'The Contribution of the FIFA World Cup and the Olympic Games to Green Economy', *Sustainability* 5(8): 3581–3600.

Rookwood, J. (2019) 'Access, Security and Diplomacy: Perceptions of Soft Power, Nation Branding and the Organisational Challenges Facing Qatar's 2022 FIFA World Cup', *Sport, Business and Management* 9(1): 26–44.

Ross, W.J. and Orr, M. (2022) 'Predicting Climate Impacts to the Olympic Games and FIFA Men's World Cups from 2022 to 2032', *Sport in Society* 25(4): 1–22.

Samuel, S. and Stubbs, W. (2013) 'Green Olympics, Green Legacies? An Exploration of the Environmental Legacies of the Olympic Games', *International Review for the Sociology of Sport* 48(4): 485–504.

Street, L., Frawley, S. and Cobourn, S. (2014) 'World Stadium Development and Sustainability', *Managing the Football World Cup* (Eds. S. Frawley and D. Adair), London: Palgrave, pp. 104–132.

Sugden, J. and Tomlinson, A. (2017) *Football, Corruption and Lies: Revisiting "Badfellas", The Book FIFA Tried to Ban*, London: Routledge.

The Guardian (2011) 'Fifa Raises $1.85bn in Broadcast Deals for 2018 and 2022 World Cups', available from: https://www.theguardian.com/football/2011/oct/27/fifa-broadcast-2018-2022-world-cups.

The Guardian (2014) 'Anti-World Cup Protests in Brazilian Cities Mark Countdown to Kick-off', available from: https://www.theguardian.com/football/2014/jun/12/anti-world-cup-protests-brazilian-cities-sao-paulo-rio-de-janeiro.

The New York Times (2016) 'In the Brazilian Rain Forest, "a White Elephant, a Big One"', available from: https://www.nytimes.com/2016/08/17/sports/-manaus-brazil-amazon-rain-forest-stadium.html.

Tomlinson, A. (2000) 'FIFA and the Men Who Made It', *Soccer & Society* 1(1): 55–71.

United 2026 (2018) 'Executive Summary – Canada, Mexico, and the United States United Bid to Host the 2026 FIFA World Cup™', available from: https://digitalhub.fifa.com/m/ba30e1119b6b29d/original/-v4cwriqezm2bauxv6xes-pdf.pdf [Accessed 11/2021].

United As One (2018) 'EIA – Executive Summary', 1–97, available from: https://digitalhub.fifa.com/m/2ce02c09f31d75e0/original/oapcqj2335fexqnlb5oc-pdf.pdf [Accessed 11/2021].

Wise, N. and Lee Ludvigsen, J.A. (2021) 'Uniting, Disuniting and Reuniting: Towards a "United" 2026', *Sport in Society* 25(4): 837–846.

Wong, D. and Chadwick, S. (2017) 'Risk and (In)Security of FIFA Football World Cups–Outlook for Russia 2018', *Sport in Society* 20(5–6): 583–598.

Yahoo News (2021) 'UNITE HERE Local 11 Urges FIFA Leadership to Choose Stadiums with Worker Protections for 2026 World Cup', available from: https://uk.news.yahoo.com/unite-local-11-urges-fifa-162700537.html?guccounter=1&guce_referrer=aHR0cHM6Ly93d3cuZ29vZ2xlLmNvbS8&guce_referrer_sig=AQAAAGpzUCD15RY3jUeIt47jSnjVBdIPUKj684TT9ZdC_9Wqk9UFm93dAZByMemjMMX3DgbnaI2w5VL-uAN4ExqPbRG_vWVDSQ306e_1lErHzi4hGSbVGS-WRrn8-xmIu-rCpg_O_fFl14BnA8n2sIUWidY1a4QTxyJb39X1z9llka69F.

Zirin, D. (2016) *Brazil's Dance with the Devil: The World Cup, The Olympics, and The Struggle for Democracy*, Chicago, IL: Haymarket Books.

4 Crime Control, Pre-Crime and Managing Risk

Trends, Technologies and Examples from Europe

Introduction

In the summer of 2016, just as the European Championship in men's football (Euro 2016) was underway in France, the *Daily Mirror* (2016), under the headline 'Euro 2016 clash between Wales and Russia upgraded to "high risk" of violence' (20 June), told the story of how over 600 extra police officers had been called into 'boost security' due to a 'high risk' of violence before the group fixture in Toulouse. The updated risk assessment followed a series of violent clashes between supporters in Lille and Marseilles earlier in the tournament. Whereas such headlines might not be entirely uncommon before or during major football tournaments (see Chapter 5), this single example is a stark indicator of authorities' and governing bodies' adoption of risk-based policies and mindsets in football (see Tsoukala, 2009).

Currently, most – if not all – professional football games and major international tournaments, as attended by thousands of supporters, pose considerable challenges for football's governing bodies, federations and clubs, law enforcements and authorities around Europe (Lee Ludvigsen, 2022; Tsoukala et al., 2016). This, coupled with the more widespread risk and future-oriented transformations in societies (Chapter 2) and within the field of criminal justice, has enabled new and increasingly anticipatory modes of governance and regulation that have transcended into and firmly embedded themselves in football cultures (Lee Ludvigsen, 2020; Spaaij, 2013). Ultimately, and compared to fans of other sports, football crowds and supporters are regularly perceived to pose a higher threat *vis-à-vis* public order and violence by football's authorities and national and international law enforcement agencies (Tsoukala et al., 2016).

This chapter examines the embeddedness of pre-emptive crime control techniques across European football settings. Significantly,

DOI: 10.4324/9781003303480-4

football fixtures may be the site for various crimes including violence, terrorism, criminal damage or street crime. Tsoukala (2009: 63) argues that it is widely accepted that the 'concern with risk and the ensuing introduction of strategies for coping with it have had a profound impact on the design and implementation of crime control policies'. This chapter thus maintains that the wider rise of risk-focused crime control policies is accurately illustrated by how football fans are governed and regulated across Europe. Furthermore, the fact that the prevention of crimes in European football, including football-related violence, is a 'Pan-European' endeavour that transcends borders (Lee Ludvigsen, 2022; Spaaij, 2013) must be viewed as crucial in this book's context: essentially, this throws light on the 'de-localized' nature of not only risk (Beck, 1992), but its management and the lessons on how to counter it.

As it proceeds, this chapter weaves together existing streams of literature and sets out to investigate how football and its supporters in the present-day are governed through anticipatory risk assessments and practices, adding further analysis through the lens of wider changes in western criminal justice systems. Particularly the impactful 'pre-crime' shift that has marked a temporal switch towards the pre-emptive anticipations of crimes that have not occurred yet – and might never occur at all (Zedner, 2007). In such context, this chapter interrogates the ways through which tournaments, specific fixtures and fans across European football are classified and categorized according to the alleged 'risk' they pose. It then discusses how the anticipations of possible terrorism and supporter violence in different football contexts mean that law enforcers, policymakers and sports governing bodies have turned towards novel technologies of monitoring and surveillance that become, as I argue, a concretized, resisted but constantly evolving facet of football's risk cultures. Such argument acquires a special sociological and criminological worth insofar it speaks to how societies' wider risk projects are in direct interaction with broader technological and cultural processes and inform the mechanisms of crime control.

Anticipating risk, crime control and 'pre-crime'

As discussed in Chapters 1 and 2, risk is commonly associated with the possibilities of *future* dangers or uncertainties (Giddens, 1999). And importantly, the term 'risk' is now commonplace in the realms of crime control and criminal justice, where it has informed – and been applied to – an array of policies and practices (Ericson and Haggerty, 1997; Mythen and Walklate, 2010). The conditions induced by the risk society have enabled significant and structural paradigm shifts. As described by Tsoukala (2008), one of the key changes within the fields of Western criminal justice systems since the twentieth century has been the shift from a 'rehabilitation-oriented' crime control model towards a 'risk-focused' model and the associated emergence of 'risk-based mindsets' (see also Tsoukala, 2013).

This emerging 'new penology' has been 'concerned with techniques to identify, classify, and manage groupings sorted by dangerousness' (Feeley and Simon, 1992: 452). One central consequence of this is the radical modification of the core objectives of crime control. Because, as compared to earlier rehabilitation-oriented policies, the new risk-focused model of criminal justice – seeking to minimize security risks – has meant that:

> social control agents are no longer seeking to defend the community against a danger posed by the commission of an offence but to protect it from the potential risk inherent in a given behaviour […] the target of social control shifts from the individual offenders to the members of the deviant, 'risk-producing' groups, who are controlled on the grounds of being suspects, in the present time, and potential offenders, *in the future*.
>
> (Tsoukala, 2008: 4, emphasis added)

The distinctive focus on controlling 'undisciplined' social groups and 'undesirable' behaviours has, importantly, 'had a considerable impact on the institutions responsible for crime management' (Tsoukala, 2009: 66). On this basis, the idea of 'pre-crime' (as contrasted by 'post-crime') is also useful to pay an important visit as an influential idea that has been picked up by criminologists and criminal justice scholars interested in security, risk and crime prevention over the past years (Zedner, 2007, 2010).

Importantly, some argue that the emergence of risk societies has encompassed a 'pre-crime' shift (Van Brakel and De Hert, 2011). The term 'pre-crime' in itself emerged in 1956, in science-fiction writer Phillip K. Dick's *The Minority Report*. This short novella focuses on the fictional criminal justice agency – called 'Precrime' – tasked with identifying and predicting future crimes before any crimes are actually committed. Though, as the main character and chief of 'Precrime' John Anderton admits, the agency's methodology proceeds with a 'basic legalistic drawback': the individuals 'Precrime' take in 'have broken no law' (Dick, 1956, cited in Zedner, 2010: 24). Similarly, in pre-crime societies, as Zedner (2007: 262) writes, crime is increasingly conceived as risk and 'the possibility of forestalling risks competes with and even takes precedence over responding to wrongs done'.

However, such a predictive outlook increasingly calls for pre-emptive policies and practices from law enforcements, private security agencies and crime control authorities that accordingly have become concerned predominantly with the *anticipation* of risks. 'Pre-crime', therefore:

> shifts the temporal perspective to anticipate and forestall that which has not yet occurred and may never do so. In a pre-crime society, there is calculation, risk and uncertainty, surveillance, precaution, prudentialism, moral hazard, prevention and, arching over all these, there is the pursuit of security.
>
> (ibid.: 262)

Consequently, 'pre-crime' captures the normative logic of preventing crimes *before* they take place. Though, this anticipatory stance as illustrated by, *inter alia*, crime predicting algorithms (Sandhu and Fussey, 2021), intensified monitoring, surveillance, exceptional legislations and 'dataveillance' has accelerated further due to the events of 9/11 (Mythen and Walklate, 2010). Simultaneously, such practices generate several questions that speak to, for example, effectiveness and proportionality (ibid.), as well as the ethical and practical concerns relevant to criminal justice realms and the wider societies (see Brayne, 2020; McCulloch and Pickering, 2009).

All of this remains important in this book's context because this forward-thinking shift and its ramifications collectively carry a high degree of relevance to football (see Tsoukala et al., 2016). Or to be more specific: it impacts both directly and indirectly the regulation and governance of football fans in the twenty-first century in the prevention of crimes, football-related violence or anti-social behaviour. Indeed, Spaaij (2013: 178) even suggests that football supporters have become a 'guinea pig' for pre-emptive modes of risk management in the present-day. Across multiple European countries, as the next sections discuss, policies, legislations and technologies are deployed in an increasingly pre-emptive and anticipatory manner with the aim of minimizing the probabilities of *future* 'undesirable' conduct and behaviour of football spectators.

Classification and categorization: governing fans through risk

Across Europe, as this chapter's introduction hinted upon, individual football matches (and supporters) are regularly classified and categorized according to 'risk' by authorities, clubs and football associations. Often, these classifications are based on selected risk characteristics and calculations. For example, the specific fixtures or individuals that are 'most likely to cause disturbances [or] most likely to be drawn into disturbances' (Giulianotti, 2009: 543). Other determining factors may include fan rivalry, a fixture's historical context, the expected presence of 'risk' fans (Spaaij, 2013) or even a relevant fixture's kick-off time.

Then again, the classification of a specific match can influence the chosen policing strategies (Giulianotti, 2009) or degree of law enforcement presence and visibility; as in the chapter's opening example where 600 extra police officers allegedly were drafted for Wales versus Russia at Euro 2016 (The Daily Mirror, 2016). Importantly, though, these classifications do not always correspond with the relevant fixture's objective risk *realities*. For example, in the UK, Hoggett and West (2020: 951) observe that in the policing of football, 'despite being "intelligence"-led, issues of "under"- and "over"-resourcing matches were observed at several of the [observed] fixtures'. Hence, they argue that the 'risk classification within the arena of football is primarily an organizational process to unlock and mobilize resources' (ibid.: 957). With regards to the risk categorization of individual supporters, James and Pearson (2015) point out that in the UK, one utilized definition of a 'risk supporter' is: 'a person, known or not, who can be regarded as posing a possible risk to public order or anti-social behaviour, whether planned or spontaneous, at or in connection with a football event' (College of Policing, 2013 cited in James and Pearson, 2015: 465). In contrast, a 'non-risk' supporter typically refers to a 'person who does not pose a risk to public order at or in connection with a football event' (Spaaij, 2013: 175).

However, such categorizations – visibly framed in terms of 'risk' – also remain highly contentious. For instance, Tsoukala et al. (2016: 172) write that 'the informal registration of fans as "risk supporters" in England and Wales takes place without the suspect or their peers being informed'. Then, when operationalized, these categorizations can impact the policing approach to 'risk supporters' on match-days (James and Pearson, 2015). From a legal perspective, James and Pearson write that the inclusion of 'anti-social behaviour' as one definitional component also means that 'it is possible that any fan who engages in boisterous conduct at a match could be seen as a risk supporter, even though they pose no risk of disorder or violence' (ibid.: 465). Furthermore, the definition makes it possible to question what exactly constitutes 'anti-social behaviour', as another controversial and contested term

(Atkinson et al., 2021). As suggested, '[t]his broad definition could lead to a larger number of supporters being termed as risk supporters' (Hester, 2021: 1190).

Yet, these processes do not necessarily apply 'solely' to national contexts. The dichotomous categorization of supporters as either 'risk' *or* 'non-risk' is also transnationally visible, on a European Union level (see Hester and Pamment, 2020; Spaaij, 2013). But still, the vagueness of such definition – focused on 'possible risks' to 'public order' and 'anti-social' behaviour as applied to the cultural context of football – means that there is 'an incredibly low threshold when much European supporter culture is based on activities which in other contexts may be seen as "anti-social", such as heavy drinking, drug use or engagement in indecent chanting' (Tsoukala et al., 2016: 172). Importantly, it is beyond the chapter's scope to provide an extensive account of all the legal and practical ramifications of these risk categorizations and the identification of individuals.[1] What remains central here is *how* these categorizing practices – by their nature and orientation – are largely pre-emptive and focus on the undesirable events or behaviours that are *possible in the future* (see Spaaij, 2013; cf. Zedner, 2007). As such, it may be contended that the established practices of risk categorization and classification identifiable across national and European football contexts, in fact, reflect the more general trajectory towards risk assessments and anticipatory endeavour which characterizes the logics underpinning of 'pre-crime' (Zedner, 2007). Further, this can concurrently be understood by making a return to the Foucauldian perspectives on risk (Spaaij, 2013; Chapter 2) which explain how pre-defined populations (supporters, in this case), through risk discourses and specific strategies, are defined as risky populations whose behaviours and movements must be regulated or require specific interventions to discipline future behaviours (Lupton, 1999). Thus, building on this, the governance of fans reveals the exercise of power across populations as facilitated by categorization strategies such as 'risk/non-risk'.

Technologies and surveillance: examples from Europe

As mentioned, the 'pre-crime' shift has been associated with intensified monitoring and surveillance techniques (Zedner, 2007). And indeed, the increasingly pre-emptive and anticipatory logics that drive football's risk management commonly manifest themselves partly through the technological solutions that are utilized to govern football supporters in the present-day. Notwithstanding, it must also be acknowledged that the contemporary surveillance technologies applied to football stadiums and spaces must be considered in the context of the post-9/11 period. Especially concerning the threat of terrorism to football and crowds, as most recently demonstrated by the attack outside *Stade de France*, in Saint-Denis just outside Paris, where France and Germany played an international fixture on 13 November 2015 (Cleland and Cashmore, 2018).[2] Resultantly, security and surveillance 'became an ever more important form of event and crowd management in football' (ibid.: 456). Notwithstanding, the realm of football – its stadiums, spaces and supporters – have historically been and continue to be employed as sites for the implementation or testing of specific surveillance technologies (Armstrong, 1998; Lee Ludvigsen, 2022; Millward et al., in press). This section showcases this by discussing some selected examples from Europe that can guide our sensemaking of how surveillant technologies govern football fans, their behaviours and mobilities, whilst simultaneously exceeding from football into more generalized contexts.

An array of 'technologies of knowledge and power' are currently deployed for the governance of football supporters in major tournaments and domestic leagues (Giulianotti and Armstrong, 2002). Not uncommonly, these technological solutions aid the aforementioned 'identification, classification and close monitoring of risk and "risky" populations' and link together biometric identification, human intelligence and CCTV (Spaaij, 2013: 167). Football games and tournaments provide authorities, private companies and security agencies with time-specific windows to trial or install high-tech surveillance technologies. For example, in Germany, the first national use of biometric facial recognition CCTV cameras occurred during the country's 2006 World Cup (Klauser, 2008). This technology 'enable[d] the images of individuals being filmed to be checked against photos that [were] already stored on "hooligan databases"' (Giulianotti, 2013: 96). Ultimately, the 2006 World Cup exemplar powerfully captures the turn towards surveillance technology in football's management of risk. For example, Eick (2011: 3300) points out that other employed surveillance technologies here encompassed 'airborne warning and control system planes (AWACS), security robots, closed circuit television surveillance (CCTV) and radio frequency chips (RFID)'. The RFID chips were set up to prevent the sale of counterfeit match tickets (ibid.). As Klauser (2008) highlights, all the 3.5 million tickets sold had embedded RFID chips that held the ticketholder's personal information and were checked electronically several times before stadium entrance. Despite emerging privacy concerns regarding this technology and the data it held, Eick (2011) writes that this World Cup's technological solutions were later extended onto the subsequent 2010 World Cup in South Africa, effectively facilitating the creation of a glocalized 'surveillant assemblage' (cf. Haggerty and Ericson, 2000).

More recently, in the UK, Fussey et al. (2021) observe how the 2017 Champions League final in the Welsh capital Cardiff was deployed as a police trial event for the use of automated facial recognition (AFR) surveillance. As touched upon, facial recognition technology involves the biometric processing of video images of individuals that are analyzed 'by a facial recognition algorithm that deciphers a subject's facial dimensions' and matched with a database (ibid.: 327). However, for critics of this technology, 'a key issue concerns purported high numbers of "false positives" generated by the system [...] when the AFR algorithm suggests a "possible match" that is inaccurate' (ibid.: 332). The aftermath of this Champions League final between Juventus and Real Madrid would likely have added fuel to such criticisms, as *BBC News* (2018) reported that: 'More than 2,000 people were wrongly identified as possible criminals by facial scanning technology at the 2017 Champions League final in Cardiff'. As a consequence of this, the civil liberties campaign group, 'Big Brother Watch', called for the technology to be scrapped due to inaccuracies and the threat to civil liberties (ibid.).

In criminal justice policies, surveillance technologies are widely utilized to collect and store data on 'those deemed to be members of suspect populations' (Zedner, 2009: 74). Similarly, football's risk management relies on constructions of profiles, data banks and systems. In the Dutch context, Spaaij (2013: 173) writes that anticipatory surveillance collates information to create profiles that 'subsequently will be used to assess risk and pre-empt behaviour'. Similarly, and more recently, Jack's (2021: 30) detailed ethnographic account of Saint Pauli supporters found that surveillance is not merely employed by the authorities to prevent illicit activities but to construct profiles on members of Ultras Saint Pauli that are 'often put into a federal database', which the fans themselves 'aren't explicitly informed if they are on'.

Whilst Chapter 5 explores fans' perceptions of risk and fear in greater depth, limited research focuses on fans' perceptions of surveillance. Yet evidence from Scottish football shows that the wide assemblage of surveillance technologies is not always positively received by supporters either (Hamilton-Smith et al., 2021). In the aftermath of the Offensive Behaviour at Football and Threatening Communications (Scotland) Act 2012, Hamilton-Smith et al. argue that some of the surveillance measures present in Scottish football – including long-range, hand-held cameras and body-worn cameras directed at 'high-risk' fans – were perceived by some fans as both 'provocative and intimidatory by targeted fans' (ibid.: 186). As they find:

> The dramatic shift in the intensity and focus of surveillance was widely felt by fans to be disproportionate and unfairly selective, with surveillance concentrated on certain behaviours, amongst certain fans, in certain stadia, for certain matches.
>
> (ibid.: 190)

Whereas I have selectively provided numerous specific exemplars or 'mini case studies' in this section, from England, Scotland, Wales, Germany and the Netherlands, the turn towards invasive surveillance techniques and novel technologies within football's risk management – clearly illustrated by my examples from different tournaments and national contexts – remain highly controversial. Whilst the vague definitions of 'high risk', 'anti-social behaviour' and 'public order' were already discussed, such technologies might also 'penetrate the life world of football supporters' and have 'important implications for supporters' civil liberties and basic rights' (Spaaij, 2013: 179). With regard to the broader context, we may therefore observe how the anticipatory shift within criminal justice, which has involved the state's turn towards 'pre-emptive endeavours' in the pursuit of increased safety and security (Zedner, 2007: 262), raises crucial questions *vis-à-vis* proportionality, ethics, effectiveness and civil liberties, as earlier stated. That is not to argue that individuals engaging in violent behaviour should not be sophistically responded to. Yet these practices can also affect many 'ordinary' football fans. Thus, the above-mentioned questions have become embedded in football, and, in various ways, my provided examples typify how surveillance technologies increasingly have been pro-actively deployed by policymakers and law enforcers subscribing to the notion that crime and disorder can be prevented *before* it takes place (Van Brakel and De Hert, 2011).

Conclusion: anticipation and contestation

To conclude, football provides spaces in which risk projects are operationalized and interact with wider processes of crime control, culture and technology. Considering football's position as a significant form of popular culture, such a contention remains both sociologically and criminologically important. This chapter does not pretend to provide an exhaustive overview of *all* risk management techniques and their (un-)intended consequences in football. Yet by drawing upon contemporary insights from European football, it remains reasonable to argue that pre-emptive risk management techniques and technologies have become a concretized yet ever-evolving facet of football (risk) cultures in the twenty-first century. Such an anticipatory stance relates to the processes existing across several European countries, which criminalize many ordinary fans as 'potential troublemakers' (Numerato, 2018: 15; Tsoukala, 2009: 58) whose presence and behaviour must be governed through risk. This notion, however, many fan groups and commentators remain highly conscious of and critical towards. Thus, whilst concretized and ever evolving; it is also resisted. Whilst many supporters are subjected to a governmental 'conduct of conduct' as one form of power, Spaaij (2013) also urges scholars to pay attention to supporters' 'counter-conduct' and modes of resistance. To better understand the outcomes of football's risk logics, he argues that:

> it is necessary to also take into account the ways in which football supporters respond to and anticipate the security and risk management technologies that are being used to conduct their behaviour
>
> (Spaaij, 2013: 179)

In the UK, for example, this is partly reflected by a Football Supporters' Association-led campaign called 'Watching Football is not a Crime',[3] which monitors the police's dealings with football fans (Numerato, 2018; Stott et al., 2019). Further, each year Football Supporters Europe leads the organization of the 'European Football Fans' Congress' which involves workshops on football-related issues including 'fair' policing (Cleland et al., 2018).[4] Across Europe, many fans have also 'long been campaigning against the introduction of a Supporters ID card' (Numerato, 2018: 15). In January 2020, a full episode of the football podcast *Football Today* was dedicated to a critical discussion of facial recognition and its future implications for football fans.[5] Taken together, there is undeniably scope for more research on how the 'pre-crime' logics engraved in football cultures are contested or resisted domestically and transnationally by fan groups, civil liberties organizations, commentators or other social movements both 'offline' and on digital platforms like podcasts, forums and social media.

Overall, this chapter has also advanced further the concept of 'pre-crime' in football and thus it provides a novel, dynamic and contemporary context in which the framework of Zedner (2007) and its key principles may be applied to. Indeed, the chapter has demonstrated how broader societal shifts and transformations within the realm of criminal justice policy (Tsoukala, 2008; Van Brakel and De Hert, 2011; Zedner, 2007) – which again can be cross-pollinated with and situated against risk theories – have meant that football supporters across Europe increasingly have become subjected to pre-emptive and anticipatory categorizations, policies and technologies that aim to reduce the probabilities of future undesirable events and behaviours. Within this continuum, fans are regularly governed through risk logics and what Tsoukala (2009: 110) calls a 'risk-focused mindset', which remain embedded in the regulation of football supporters. Notwithstanding, all this carries a significance beyond football, as the risk-related practices, policies and applications discussed throughout simultaneously tell us something about late modernity's preoccupation with the mitigation and management of *future* and de-localized crime risks and pre-defined (but vague) 'risky' populations or social groups.

Notes

1 For this, consult e.g., James and Pearson (2015, 2016).
2 This attack was a part of the coordinated attacks across Paris on that day, which killed 130 people overall (Cleland and Cashmore, 2018: 455).
3 See: https://thefsa.org.uk/news/watching-football-is-not-a-crime/ (Accessed 01/2022).
4 See: https://www.fanseurope.org/en/fans-congress.html (Accessed 11/2021).
5 See: https://www.footballtodaypodcast.com/post/facial-recognition-football-in-the-age-of-surveillance (Accessed 11/2021).

References

Armstrong, G. (1998) *Football Hooligans: Knowing the Score*, Oxford/New York: Berg.

Atkinson, C., McBride, M. and Moore, A. (2021) 'Pitched! Informants and the Covert Policing of Football Fans in Scotland', *Policing and Society* 31(7): 863–877.

BBC News (2018) '2,000 Wrongly Matched with Possible criminals at Champions League', available from: https://www.bbc.co.uk/news/uk-wales-south-west-wales-44007872.

Beck, U. (1992) *Risk Society: Towards a New Modernity*, London: Sage.

Brayne, S. (2020) *Predict and Surveil: Data, Discretion, and the Future of Policing*, Oxford: Oxford University Press.

Cleland, J. and Cashmore, E. (2018) 'Nothing Will be the Same Again After the Stade de France Attack: Reflections of Association Football Fans on Terrorism, Security and Surveillance', *Journal of Sport and Social Issues* 42(6): 454–469.

Cleland, J., Doidge, M., Millward, P., and Widdop, P. (2018) *Collective Action and Football Fandom: A Relational Sociological Approach*, New York: Palgrave.

Eick, V. (2011) 'Lack of Legacy? Shadows of Surveillance after the 2006 FIFA World Cup in Germany', *Urban Studies* 48(15): 3329–3345.

Ericson, R. and Haggerty, K. (1997) *Policing the Risk Society*, Toronto: University of Toronto Press.

Feeley, M.M. and Simon, J. (1992) 'The New Penology: Notes on the Emerging Strategy of Corrections and Its Implications', *Criminology* 30(4): 449–474.

Fussey, P., Davies, B. and Innes, M. (2021) '"Assisted" Facial Recognition and the Reinvention of Suspicion and Discretion in Digital Policing', *British Journal of Criminology* 61(2): 325–344.

Giddens, A. (1999) 'Risk and Responsibility', *The Modern Law Review* 62(1): 1–35.

Giulianotti, R. (2009) 'Risk and Sport: An Analysis of Sociological Theories and Research Agendas', *Sociology of Sport Journal* 26(4): 540–556.

Giulianotti, R. (2013) 'Six Security Legacies of Major Sporting Events', *ICSS Journal* 1(1): 95–101.

Giulianotti, R. and Armstrong, G. (2002) 'Avenues of Contestation. Football Hooligans Running and Ruling Urban Spaces', *Social Anthropology* 10(2): 211–238.

Haggerty, K.D. and Ericson, R.V. (2000) 'The Surveillant Assemblage', *British Journal of Sociology* 51(4): 605–622.

Hester, R. and Pamment, N. (2020) '"It's Become Fashionable": Practitioner Perspectives on Football Hooliganism Involving Young People', *International Journal of Police Science & Management* 22(4): 366–377.

Hester, R. (2021) 'Assessing the UK Football Policing Unit Funding of Football Banning Orders in Times of Policing Austerity', *Policing* 15(2): 1188–1201.

Hoggett, J. and West, O. (2020) 'Police Liaison Officers at Football: Challenging Orthodoxy through Communication and Engagement', *Policing* 14(4): 945–961.

Jack, M. (2021) '"You Call This Democracy? FC Saint Pauli Supporters, Football Chants, and the Police', *Football and Popular Culture: Singing Out from the Stands* (Eds. S. Millar, M. Power, P. Widdop, D. Parnell and J. Carr), London: Routledge, pp. 25–38.

James, M. and Pearson, G. (2015) 'Public Order and the Rebalancing of Football Fans' Rights: Legal Problems with Pre-Emptive Policing Strategies and Banning Orders', *Public Law* 3: 458–475.

James, M. and Pearson, G. (2016) 'Legal Responses to Football Crowd Disorder and Violence in England and Wales', *Legal Responses to Football Hooliganism in Europe* (Eds. A. Tsoukala, G. Pearson and P.T.M. Coenen), The Hague: Springer, pp. 35–52.

Klauser, F. (2008) 'Spatial Articulations of Surveillance at the FIFA World Cup 2006 in Germany', *Technologies of Insecurity* (Eds. K. Aas, H.O. Gundhus and H.M. Lomell), London: Routledge, pp. 61–80.

Lee Ludvigsen, J.A. (2020) 'The "Troika of Security": Merging Retrospective and Futuristic "Risk" and "Security" Assessments before Euro 2020', *Leisure Studies* 39(6): 844–858.

Lee Ludvigsen, J.A. (2022) *Sport Mega-Events, Security and Covid-19: Securing the Football World*, London/New York: Routledge.

Lupton, D. (1999) *Risk*, Routledge: London.

McCulloch, J. and Pickering, S. (2009) 'Pre-Crime and Counter-Terrorism: Imagining Future Crime in the "War on Terror"', *The British Journal of Criminology* 49(5): 628–645.

Millward, P., Lee Ludvigsen, J.A. and Sly, J. (in press) *Sport and Crime: Towards a Critical Criminology of Sport*, Routledge.

Mythen, G. and Walklate, S. (2010) 'Pre-Crime, Regulation, and Counter-Terrorism: Interrogating Anticipatory Risk: Gabe Mythen and Sandra Walklate Explore the Extent to Which Risk Is Being Utilised More Intensively in the Development of Crime Control Policies', *Criminal Justice Matters* 81(1): 34–36.

Hamilton-Smith, N., McBride, M. and Atkinson, C. (2021) 'Lights, Camera, Provocation? Exploring Experiences of Surveillance in the Policing of Scottish Football', *Policing and Society* 31(2), 179–194.

Numerato, D. (2018) *Football Fans, Activism and Social Change*, London: Routledge.

Sandhu, A. and Fussey, P. (2021) 'The "Uberization of Policing"? How Police Negotiate and Operationalise Predictive Policing Technology', *Policing and Society* 31(1): 66–81.

Spaaij, R. (2013) 'Risk, Security and Technology: Governing Football Supporters in the Twenty-First Century', *Sport in Society* 16(2):167–183.

Stott, C., Pearson, G. and West, O. (2020) 'Enabling an Evidence-Based Approach to Policing Football in the UK', *Policing* 14(4): 977–994.

The Daily Mirror (2016) 'Euro 2016 Clash between Wales and Russia Upgraded to "High Risk" of Violence', available from: https://www.mirror.co.uk/news/uk-news/euro-2016-clash-between-wales-8234229.

Tsoukala, A. (2008) 'Security, Risk and Human Rights: A Vanishing Relationship?', *CEPS Special Reports*: 1–17.

Tsoukala, A. (2009) *Football Hooliganism in Europe: Security and Civil Liberties in the Balance*, Basingstoke: Springer.

Tsoukala, A. (2013) 'Controlling Football-Related Violence in France: Law and Order Versus the Rule of Law', *Sport in Society* 16(2): 140–150.

Tsoukala, A., Pearson, G. and Coenen, P.T.M. (2016) 'Legal Responses to Football 'Hooliganism' in Europe – Introduction', *Legal Responses to Football Hooliganism in Europe* (Eds. A. Tsoukala, G. Pearson and P.T.M. Coenen), The Hague: Springer, pp. 1–17.

Van Brakel, R. and De Hert, P. (2011) 'Policing, Surveillance and Law in a Pre-Crime Cociety: Understanding the Consequences of Technology Based Strategies', *Technology Led Policing* 20: 165–192.

Zedner, L. (2007) 'Pre-Crime and Post-Criminology?', *Theoretical Criminology* 11(2): 261–281.
Zedner, L. (2009) *Security*, London/New York: Routledge.
Zedner, L. (2010) 'Pre-Crime and Pre-Punishment: A Health Warning: Lucia Zedner Calls for Restraint', *Criminal Justice Matters* 81(1): 24–25.

5 Risk Perceptions, Dangerousness and the Media

Introduction

As Chapter 2 unpacked, one of the defining characteristics of modern risk societies is individuals' enhanced awareness of the risks and uncertainties that are 'out there' and the other real or perceived dangers to their safety. As reflected by recent years' events – perhaps most notably the 2015 *Stade de France* terrorist attack (Cleland and Cashmore, 2018), the 'riots' and supporter violence at Euro 2016 (The Independent, 2016), Covid-19 and the disorder inside and around Wembley for London's Euro 2020 final (Lee Ludvigsen, 2022) – attending football matches or tournaments can involve considerable risks to one's health and safety. The creation of safe environments for athletes, spectators and citizens is hence located at the core of football's risk management strategies (Cleland, 2019). However, do fans feel safe upon attending football matches or events? How do fans respond to risk? All this provides the backdrop for this chapter, which consciously weaves together the empirical findings from the existing literature streams on risk perceptions amongst football supporters. More specifically, this chapter first aims to explore how football fans, as a diverse but transnationally significant social group, cope with and negotiate risks: whether fans, upon attending football, feel afraid, anxious, safe or display resilience.

Notwithstanding, in this context, the mass media's communication of risks is also highly relevant to consider, since the media can influence fans' risk subjectivities. For example, Cleland (2019: 145) reminds us that:

> One prominent factor in the presentation of risk is through the mass media [...] which can result in a sense of panic amongst civilians that creates even greater levels of anxiety and alterations to every day behavior through the perception that they could fall victim to terrorism.

DOI: 10.4324/9781003303480-5

Given this crucial *risk perception-media* nucleus, this chapter's second aim is to investigate how the narratives and discourses – as communicated through the media – co-exist with and influence individuals' risk perceptions and in the broader social construction of fear and 'dangerousness' in football (see Tsoukala, 2008).

The media plays a central role in the communication of risk (Bakir, 2010). Ahead of sporting events, it is now established that sensitive themes such as 'terrorism, fear, risk and surveillance' (Atkinson and Young, 2012: 287, see also Millward et al., in press) dominate the media coverage and headlines. However, not uncommonly, fans are also presented as 'dangerous' or 'at risk' populations that may pose a threat to wider communities and the public order. To explore this further, this chapter zooms in on and analytically explores the unique case of English Premier League's (EPL) 'Project Restart'. 'Project Restart' refers to the complex resumption of the EPL following the Covid-19 related suspension of the 2019/2020 season (between March and June 2020). This process was nicknamed 'Project Restart' in the media because *restarting* the EPL – as postponed on 13 March 2020 – was the end-goal of the process. Indeed, after a 100-day long break, the EPL returned on 17 June 2020 when Aston Villa hosted Sheffield United behind 'closed doors'.[1] Yet, as the chapter argues, this exceptional case also reveals an exemplar of how fans, through discourses and communications in the media, are commonly framed as 'potential trouble-makers' (Numerato, 2018; see also Chapter 4) and to pose what I call a 'double risk'. That is, in the coronavirus pandemic's context, fans were not solely framed as risks to *public order*, but to *public health* too.

Fans' perceptions of risk, fear and (in)security

This section examines fans' perceptions of risk, fear and insecurity with a particular focus on the themes of acceptance of, and resistance towards, risks. The ability to perceive and avoid harmful environments is biologically inherited and usually considered necessary for human survival and life (Baker et al., 2007). Furthermore, as Lupton (1999: 107) asserts, 'many aspects of people's lives are influenced by their awareness of risk and the responsibilities involved in avoiding risks'. While individuals construct risk knowledge in their everyday lives (ibid.), perceptions and awareness of risk are not confined to people's 'everyday' life or settings (Lupton and Tulloch, 2002). In football, fans – when attending football matches or events – will naturally make up their own unique and subjective risk perceptions. Such perceptions may also impact fans' behaviours or even their desire to attend football. Indeed, some even suggest that 'perceptions of risk are as important – if not more so – than the actuality of the risks we face, as perceptions often determine behaviour' (Durodie, 2007: 76 cited in Taylor and Toohey, 2015: 378).

Tarlow (2002) argues that it is expected by and in the best interest of event visitors, except for allocentric adventurers, to visit safe event environments. In football's context, such contention may, however, be complicated by the incidents referred to in the chapter's introduction and of course the Covid-19 pandemic, which has impacted sports enthusiasts' outlooks on safety and protective measures (Perić et al., 2021). As discussed later too, the media also plays a pivotal role in the amplification of subjective risk perceptions before major football tournaments. The mass media reminds (potential) event visitors about the potential threats and risks that are associated with sport (Atkinson and Young, 2012).

Yet the question orienting this section relates to how exactly football fans perceive risks. Within the sociology of sport, there is currently limited research exploring how fans perceive risk, fear or (in)security and, indeed, those measures taken to provide safety. Though, this research lacuna is also identifiable in the wider literature. For example, Stevens and Vaughan-Williams (2017: 96) write that 'little is actually known about public attitudes towards the full spectrum of security threats' that individuals are faced with or perceive. Others highlight that:

> while much has been said about security discourses and techniques, far less has been said of the ways in which practical security measures are experienced, felt and managed by individuals and groups.
>
> (Crawford and Hutchinson, 2016: 1185)

These arguments may be imported into this chapter's discussion and, as Hassan (2016: 1047) argues in relation to sporting events – not exclusively related to football: 'an often over-looked consequence [of threats] has been their impact on potential attendees deciding to travel to attend [events]'.

There is, however, a smaller set of studies that examine fans' or football tourists' risk and safety perceptions, which provide some crucial empirical insights into fans' risk-related responses. For example, in the case of South Korea and Japan's co-hosted 2002 World Cup, Toohey et al. (2003) use a questionnaire survey (n = 277) to find that 'most respondents' attending this World Cup (76%) either felt 'safe' or 'very safe' in context of heightened terrorist threats in the immediate post-9/11 climate. Further, Toohey et al. contend that security risks and safety concerns were not a major factor in attendees' decision to attend less than a year after the mentioned 9/11 attacks. Merely six percent of the respondents claimed that the visibility of security and safety measures reduced their level of enjoyment whilst attending the World Cup (ibid.). Moreover, following the South Africa's 2010 World Cup, where urban and local crime emerged as *the* key concern pre-event (Wong and Chadwick, 2017), George and Swart (2012) examined perceptions of crime-related risks. By drawing from a survey with 398 respondents, they concluded that the majority of attendees left the country with positive perceptions towards crime and felt safe throughout their stay.

Away from World Cup case studies, Lee Ludvigsen and Millward (2020) explore EPL supporters' responses to security threats following a 2016 match-day stadium evacuation. Here, we found that supporters appreciated security officials' management of the incident and how fans' safety was prioritized with the decision to postpone the match to a later date. Supporters also saw how the incident, which fortunately never materialized into a tragedy, would likely lead to an enhanced focus on security and risk management at future events. Ultimately, we argued that: 'Supporters seemingly recognize that events are sites "at risk"' (ibid.: 17). Such findings remain important and connect with two other sociological studies in this field. In the aftermath of the 2015 *Stade de France* attack, Cleland and Cashmore (2018) find that football fans were mostly supportive of security initiatives and displayed a willingness to cooperate with authorities for the shared desire of safe events. Again, it is noticeable how the researchers also find an *acceptance* among fans that football potentially may be the site of terrorist attacks, given the sport's global profile and status as the most popular sport in the world. Meanwhile, drawing upon responses from 1,015 sport fans concerning their own experiences of risk, security and terrorism in sport, Cleland's (2019) findings suggest that sport fans have learnt to live with risks in their daily routines.[2] Cleland employs Beck's risk society as a theoretical framework and argues that:

> One of the conclusions to be drawn from this [study] is that the risk society advanced by Beck (1992) is present in the minds of a significant number of fans across a variety of sports with a greater awareness and consciousness of risk negatively impacting those fans who are more fearful of a terrorist attack occurring. [...]

this has subsequently led to the development of more risk averse behaviors.

(Cleland, 2019: 150)

Whilst the majority fans in Cleland's (2019) study displayed resistance, defiance and pragmatism by continuing their existing routines *despite* the real and perceived security risks, it should also be noted that 20% of the respondents felt some risk, whilst nine percent felt 'a lot' of risk upon attending sports events.

When making sense of this in relation to the risk societies' key tenets (Chapter 2), these findings appear to be indicative of – and say something about how individuals in risk societies adapt to and appreciate the notion that risks are now 'everywhere', outside of their own control and how individuals mark their resistance by not allowing the perceived or objectively real risks to deter their attendance or enjoyment. This connects with Taylor and Toohey's (2007: 101) assertion that sport mega-events can be understood as 'sites of resistance, with attendees showing defiance and resistance to the possibility of violence through their mere presence at the sporting fixture'. Indeed, this speaks to what Beck (1992: 19, emphasis added) highlighted himself:

> more and more aspects of our lives are framed by an awareness of the dangers confronting humankind at the individual, local and global level, and the need to *develop strategies to confront these dangers.*

Arguably, the resistance, defiance and pragmatism displayed by individual fans (Cleland, 2019) demonstrate reflexive techniques through which dangers and risks are strategically confronted. Yet Cleland's findings also demonstrate how the fears of risks, in fact, impact some fans' routines. Certain fans in his study, for example, stated that they had begun to look out for 'suspicious behaviours' or display extra consciousness in crowded spaces (p. 149). For Cleland, the latter can also be seen as connected to the mass media's communications of risk because the:

> message the media convey can strongly influence the thoughts and behaviors of people who remain fearful of the unknown and the subsequent lack of control they feel about the ways in which they go about their lives.

(ibid.: 149)

Collectively, the empirical findings drawn from pre-existing studies make it arguable that, in the current time, increasingly reflexive football fans have become somewhat acclimatized to relevant security risks and their accompanying measures. This does not mean that fans do not display fear or insecurity, but that they seem to accept that risks are a part of the match-day experience and football culture as within society as a whole.

More broadly, this corresponds with Zedner's (2009: 125) claim that anti-terror security measures – many of which are present in football – including surveillance, identity checks, searches and mass data collection, have become so 'deeply embedded that they scarcely any longer merit notice'. Visitors of football events are not uncommonly tourists and, interestingly, similar arguments emerge from the tourism literature. Some contend that tourists have become so habituated to security procedures emanating already from the airport stage, that these procedures become expected in other areas of the travelling experience (Feickert et al., 2006). Ultimately, the present-day international tourist experience is much synonymous with surveillance, risk and security (Lisle, 2016; Morgan and Pritchard, 2005; Urry and Larsen, 2011).[3]

The apparent degree of normalization and acceptance of security risks, however, does not mean that all football fans accept all security measures at face value (Lee Ludvigsen, 2022; Millward et al., in press) and importantly, risks are still subjectively felt on an individual level. Whereas many fans clearly expect a presence of security and safety measures directed towards the prevention of risk, not all fans will, as Chapter 4 discussed, support draconian measures that may hinder the match-day experience, rituals or atmospheres (Numerato, 2018). Overall, the existing research demonstrates how some fans consciously resist and seemingly 'get on' with risks, whereas other fans articulate fear and risk aversion (Cleland, 2019; Lee Ludvigsen and Millward, 2020). However, it may still be argued that further research is needed, which qualitatively appreciates fans' risk responses and how they cope with and negotiate risks and how cultures, gender, disability, race and sexuality impact this.

Such research must also consider Covid-19's social implications. Müller et al. (2021: 8) remind us that: 'Where previously a crowd of people packed into a stadium or partying on a public square after medal ceremonies induced joy and a celebratory mood, mass gatherings now install fear'. The pandemic has meant that the mere proximity between people poses a risk to public health and safety. It has also brought about new considerations for football bodies and organizers related to ensuring social distancing, hygiene, face masks and communicating crucial Covid-19 information (Lee Ludvigsen, 2022). For such research, anecdotal evidence suggests that frames from the earlier literature can be re-applied. 'We've got to get on with things', one supporter interviewed by Sky News (2021) outside Arsenal's Emirates Stadium commented, as the Omicron variant of Covid-19 spread globally and re-elevated concerns associated with social contact in December 2021. Another fan, meanwhile, seemed to accept that: 'Being around lots and lots of people is far more dangerous' than not attending, but that a balance was needed 'between keeping safe and your mental health and your wellbeing' (ibid.). In all, the assertion that little is known about 'how the public perceives risks associated with emerging infectious diseases' (Dryhurst et al., 2020: 995) can be echoed in 'post-pandemic' football.

The media, communications of risk and the construction of 'dangerousness'

Now, I turn to examine how risk is communicated *through,* or *by,* the media in football's context. Here, some context is required first. As previously mentioned, media headlines, discourses and communications have the capacity to shape individuals' subjective risk perceptions. For example, what an individual reads about online or watches on television can directly impact how the same individual 'experiences, responds to and feels security measures in their everyday life' (Crawford and Hutchinson, 2016: 1196). Ultimately, I seek to discuss in this section how football fans' risk perceptions may be influenced by risk communications in the media. Yet the chapter also argues that the media is not merely reminding football fans about risks and threats to their own safety. The coverage and discourses by or through the media may also contribute towards the framing of fans as 'at risk' or 'dangerous' social groups.

Beck would argue that the mass media is one site for the social construction, social contestation and social criticism of risks (Cottle, 1998). Initially, Beck (1992: 23) positioned the mass media as 'in charge of defining risk' together with scientific and legal professionals. Later, the importance of the media continued to (re-)appear in his work in regard to how risk staging had become an 'increasingly common feature of the modern multi-media landscape and one which involves a variety of institutions and actors' (Mythen, 2018: 22). Importantly, the media's 'staging' or definition of risk transcends into the world of football, and whereas mass media coverage may drive football's governing bodies, tournament organizers or authorities to implement specific risk management strategies, it may also shape the public's perceptions. In recent years, this has meant that 'security risks, particularly in relation to terrorism threats and violence, has been a mainstay of media reporting on mega-events such as the World Cup and the Olympics' (Taylor and Toohey, 2015: 388). This, despite the fact – and paradox – that there is a 'low risk' of actual terrorism incidents taking place during sport mega-events (ibid.: 379). Partly for this reason, Atkinson and Young (2012) argue that post-9/11 sport mega-events – due to mass mediation – represent 'fabricated zones of risk', where terrorism risks constitute what Jean Baudrillard called 'non-events'. According to the Atkinson and Young (2012), the mass media coverage before sporting events creates an imaginary perception of events as 'zones of terror' (p. 296). Yet usually 'non-events' do *not* live up to its assigned status in the media, hence:

> pre-emptive warnings about imminent terrorist violence at major Games are like movie previews or trailers that are aired constantly (stirring the emotions), but the final movie is neither eventually produced nor shown to audiences.
>
> (ibid.)

Naturally, all this speaks to how the mass mediation of risks, threats and dangers to people's safety may be dramatized or magnified and, in part, are socially constructed and defined (Beck, 1992; see Chapter 2). For Atkinson and Young (2012: 296), the 'sport-terrorism discourses and practices in the West conceal the fact that there is barely any sport-related terrorism at all'. Such media coverage is not uncommonly supplemented by authorities and security officials commenting, in the media or press releases, on how they are planning for 'worst-case scenarios' that are in fact uncontrollable (Boyle and Haggerty, 2012).

Not too dissimilarly, Poulton (2005: 31) observes that, in the run-up to major international football tournaments, there is a pronounced tendency of 'alarmist prophesies' and media amplification of the prospects of football-related violence or 'hooliganism'. All this remains important because this illustrates how football is surrounded by risk-fuelled discourses that can come to shape or impact fans' awareness of risks. However, whilst the ways in which the media communicates risks may remind football fans about the diverse dangers associated with match-day attendance, the media's coverage (or statements that are communicated through the media) may also serve to socially construct football fans as 'at risk' or potentially 'dangerous' populations that require intervention (Chapter 4).

As Tsoukala's (2008) analysis of British media coverage and framing of 'football hooligans' and 'terrorism' suggests, the social construction of threat means that 'football hooligans' are defined as a dangerous 'other' that is opposed to – and a deviant social enemy of – the wider community. Following Tsoukala, this can be understood as a boundary-creating process in which social problems and groups are defined. Yet as she notes, '[t]his ordinary defining process is strengthened in times of crisis when the community and/or its values are, or are thought to be, in danger' (p. 141). Importantly, however, the boundary-creating process may invite and allow for the 'introduction of a series of exceptional measures against football hooligans' (p. 149) to counter their 'dangerousness'. Whereas Tsoukala is principally concerned with 'hooligans', the media-related processes she analyses have implications for the next section's case study. Here, I explain how 'ordinary fans', during Covid-19, were framed as what I call a 'double risk' to football's resumption after the EPL's Covid-suspension.

Fans as a 'double risk' to football's return: Covid-19 and Project Restart

The next section sheds a light on how fans, through media discourses, were framed as a 'double risk' to football's resumption following the Covid-19 suspension in the case of the EPL's 'Project Restart'. For contextual purposes, the EPL has, as a professional football league – since its establishment in 1992 – been subject to a substantial amount of social research (e.g., Millward, 2011; Webber, 2021). Essentially, the league's actions and images are transmitted globally to 188 countries, whilst the league's players, staff and club owners are drawn from transnational markets and networks making the league a highly globalized enterprise (Millward, 2011). The league's broadcasting rights for matches between 2019 and 2022 – currently shared by Sky Sports, BT Sports and Amazon – were sold for £4.464 billion (BBC, 2018) demonstrating the enormous interest in, and economic value of, the EPL's images. With a league and its competing clubs located between commercial and global elites and powerful actors, Webber (2021: 599) highlights that 'a transnational assemblage of owners, broadcasters, corporate sponsors and supporters have coalesced around these elite sporting institutions to form a new leisure class at the top of English football'. Simultaneously, this underpins the overarching perspective locating the EPL as an interesting case for the analyses of social issues including risk.

Whereas the EPL's smooth running and organization have been affected by external events or crises previously, including the 2007/2008 financial crisis and the 2010 volcanic ash cloud which disrupted European airspace (including flows of transnational fans) (Millward, 2011), it has never been as seriously disrupted as it was in the spring of 2020. Much like in the rest of the world, the Covid-19 pandemic caused an unprecedented crisis for the EPL. To prevent and contain the virus spread, mass gatherings and football leagues worldwide, including the EPL, were postponed or called off (Clarkson et al., 2022).

The EPL was suspended on 13 March 2020. At this point, other competitions – including the Italian Serie A and Champions League matches – had already been postponed or taken place behind 'closed doors' (Moore, 2021). In the UK, however, sporting events had been staged in front of mass crowds: Liverpool's Champions League fixture versus Atletico Madrid took place as normal on the 11 March, and the Cheltenham Festival horse race was staged in front of 250,000 spectators between 10 and 13 March (ibid.). In spite of this, Manchester City's home game against Arsenal (to be staged on 11 March) was postponed after reports of a number of players who had to self-isolate (BBC, 2020). Initially, the EPL with the Football Association (FA), the English Football League and the FA Women's Super League collectively suspended football until 4 April, though this was later extended (Clarkson et al., 2022). At this stage, reports also emerged of players and staff that had been infected by the virus, meaning that stadiums and training grounds were also closed in line with workplace restrictions and nationwide social distancing measures as the UK wide lockdown was enforced on 23 March 2020 (The Guardian, 2020). Upon the EPL's suspension, 92 out of 380 games still remained to be played to finish the 2019/2020 season and the league remained suspended between 13 March and 17 June 2020.

In the absence of *live* football actions, the EPL's constant media coverage continued apace. However, in the UK, the return of football was not merely framed as a social good that could 'lift the spirits of the nation' during the first lockdown (Moore, 2021: 48). The remainder of this discussion draws from an analysis of 84 media articles published online between 13 March and 1 July 2020 that discussed or reported on 'Project Restart'.[4] Here, one surfacing and dominant frame surrounding 'Project Restart' was the alleged risk of fans to the successful behind-closed-doors resumption of the EPL. Indeed, even before Covid-19, football matches were already 'some of the most tightly regulated social spaces in British society' (James and Pearson, 2016: 39). However, as the 'Project Restart' plans advanced, policing concerns were repeatedly articulated. Even though the planned games would be played behind closed doors – hence, without fans *inside* the stadiums – the media coverage of 'Project Restart' revealed a wider fear of fans congregating in crowds *outside* the stadiums or in other spaces, and thereby breaching public health measures. As argued here, this notion can be seen in the context of the broader criminalization of football supporters (Numerato, 2018) and the socially constructed images of football supporters as possible dangers to the public (Tsoukala, 2008). Yet in this case, fans were seemingly framed as a 'double risk', to both public order and health.

Overall, the plans to resume the EPL was surrounded by a 'language of fear around fans' (The Independent, 2020). This mostly related to (largely unevidenced) suggestions maintaining that fans, on match-days, would congregate outside stadiums, gather in crowds and thereby breach the UK's legally enforced social distancing measures at the time. For example, *The Telegraph* (2020) ran the headline 'Football's return? Police want season called off altogether if fans gather to watch games'. Meanwhile, the *Daily Mirror* (2020a) reported that: 'Police consulted over fears Liverpool fans could mob streets on day Reds win title'.[5] Here, it was reported that 'until the issue is resolved, it threatens to be a stumbling block to re-starting the Premier League season' (ibid.). Other media accounts claimed that: 'A senior police official in the Midlands has said that the Premier League's Project Restart is "fraught with risk" for fans and police officers' (The Times, 2020). Collectively, these exemplars are illustrative of how fans – even *without* the opportunity to enter the stadiums – were considered as likely to gather and therefore also relocate policing efforts, breach social distancing measures and compose a risk to the police and wider public. As such, staging EPL fixtures at neutral venues was discussed as one potential solution to the prospect of fans congregating (The Daily Mail, 2020). In a response to this proposal, the North Wales Police and Crime Commissioner, Arfon Jones stated that: 'The push to play at neutral venues is nonsense and is not supported by evidence', and that: 'At the end of the day, there are not going to be any fans at the grounds' (quoted in Liverpool Echo, 2020). He also added: 'They are basing neutral venues on the fact that fans may turn up to the ground, but there is no reason to suspect they will' (ibid.). The neutral venue proposal was also opposed by EPL clubs. The league's Chief Executive, Richard Masters, commented:

> Obviously from the authorities' perspective, some authorities think that playing those matches at approved stadia, not the home

venues, is the safest way forward [...] It's also about ensuring the fans [...] *about creating as little risk as possible in relation to fans coming to attend the matches outside a behind closed doors environment* [...] We have spoken to our clubs today about this topic. I have said it's a live topic and we will continue to discuss it. It's not a matter of convincing, because we need to listen to each other [...] I think some of our clubs would argue that in relation to policing their own fans that they have a good relationship with them, and that they encourage their own fans not to turn up outside their home venues while they're playing behind closed doors.

(quoted in *The Daily Mirror*, 2020b, emphasis added)

However, it is necessary to critically question the possible reasons why the risk of fans gathering was so frequently communicated through the media. Potentially, these concerns were based on the incident where Paris Saint Germain fans congregated outside *Parc de Princes* for the team's Champions League fixture against Borussia Dortmund played behind closed doors on 11 March 2020. Importantly, however, this occurred before France had banned public gatherings of more than 100 people as a Covid-19 response (Reddy, 2020). The discourses also reveal an *assumption* holding that fans would breach social distancing measures. Such an assumption, however, was based on scant evidence when framed as an obstacle to the EPL's safe restart. As Labour MP for West Derby, Ian Byrne said: '[the] framing of football fans by some parties during this [Covid] crisis and around issues of restarting our wonderful game is concerning and harks back to past perceptions from another age' (quoted in Reddy, 2020).

Overall, it can be contended that the media discourses surrounding 'Project Restart' represented a continuation of the construction of football fans as an 'at risk' or potentially 'dangerous' social group. Such a stance has impacted regulations and policing realities (Chapter 4). As James and Pearson (2016: 39) submit, a number of legislative provisions and policing strategies have ensured that 'football spectators are prohibited from many actions that would be permitted in other social, crowd or sporting situations'. Furthermore, this demonstrates how, in football, the media's communications of risk relate both to the risks that fans are exposed to *and* fans as potentially 'dangerous', 'disruptive' or 'high-risk' groups. Concerning the latter, the 'Project Restart' example, in distinctive ways, served to reinforce longstanding views of fans as 'potential troublemakers' (Numerato, 2018) who must be policed and governed even without access to the closed-off stadiums. Whereas the discourses maintaining that fans would disrupt 'Project Restart' were resisted by some critical voices (Reddy, 2020), it is arguable that the assumptions upon which these discourses were based on reflect a broader trend speaking to the framing and criminalization of fans (Numerato, 2018).

Whilst the case of 'Project Restart' served as a continuation of media discourses that reinforce the social constructions of fans' alleged and potential 'dangerousness' (Tsoukala, 2008), the analysis of 'Project Restart' also extends our understanding of how the 'risk' supposedly posed by fans was reconfigured in line with the Covid-19 health crisis. On this occasion, fans were not only a potential risk to public order, but to the public health crisis of Covid-19 too. As communicated through the media, fans allegedly posed what I advance as a 'double risk'. As I discussed elsewhere, a similar trend also emerged before England's Euro 2020 fixture against Scotland, where the media discourses, again, focused on the 'double risk' of fans as threats to both public order and public health during the pandemic (Lee Ludvigsen, 2022). Taken together, this demonstrates how the media provides a platform through which the 'riskification' of football is entrenched, constructed and amplified, and where separate risks can be *bundled together*.

Conclusion

This chapter has woven together two inter-linked aspects of risk in football. First, it discussed how fans perceive risks, fear and insecurity. Second, it examines how the media's risk communications, and the coverage of potential risks may impact fans' perceptions of security risks, threats and dangers. Both of these aspects, fundamentally, compose a central element of Beck's risk society thesis (Chapter 2). Through an analysis of the EPL's 'Project Restart' in 2020 (during Covid-19), I also demonstrated how fans, during the pandemic, were framed as a 'double risk' to *public health* and *public order* through the media. To 'Project Restart's' safety and success, fans were framed as a potentially disruptive force. In a way, such discourses represent another mechanism through which fans are governed through risk, as Chapter 4 discussed.

Ultimately, this chapter forwards two main arguments. First, the mass media coverage of risks to major football events and sport is not merely focused on those 'external' threats that fans could be exposed to. They also revolve around the 'danger' or (double) 'risk' that fans, supposedly, pose to the social order and wider communities. Second, from making sense of the empirical findings from existing studies

(Cleland, 2019; Cleland and Cashmore, 2018; Lee Ludvigsen and Millward, 2020), it may be contended that football fans' perceptions, reflexive awareness and acceptance of risks in football echoes individuals' increased reflexivity and risk consciousness in modern societies and individuals' strategic confrontation of risks (Beck, 1992; Lupton and Tulloch, 2002). As argued, football fans seem increasingly normalized to, and accepting of, the real and perceived threats and perils associated with football attendance (Cleland, 2019; Lee Ludvigsen and Millward, 2020). Whereas some fans' may alter their behaviour or way of living as a result, other fans simultaneously confront, resist and 'get on' with these security and safety risks by attending and thereby not allowing potential risks to determine their way of life. Thus, as a final remark, it can be contended that football's spaces, cultures and events must be approached seriously as key sites and contested domains where individuals experience, negotiate, avoid and even resist the different risks and dangers of the modern day.

Notes

1 This refers to fixtures where spectators are not allowed inside the stadium.
2 The respondents in this research are not limited to football fans, however.
3 A point well illustrated by the inclusion of a chapter dedicated to 'Risks and Futures' in the third edition of *The Tourist Gaze* (2011). A chapter which was non-apparent in the book's earlier editions. In the current era of global risks, Urry and Larsen (2011: 221, original emphasis) observe that 'tourist places can thus attract tourists *and* terrorists'.
4 Adopting the approach of Atkinson and Young (2012) no rigid selection criteria guided my sampling. Instead, the sampled articles had to address the EPL, 'Project Restart' or English football and COVID-19. The terms informing the searches were: 'Premier League'; 'English Premier League'; 'COVID-19' and 'Project Restart'.
5 Here, 'The Reds' refer to Liverpool FC, who would win 2019/20 season of the EPL.

References

Atkinson, M. and Young, K. (2012) 'Shadowed by the Corpse of War: Sport Spectacles and the Spirit of Terrorism', *International Review for the Sociology of Sport* 47(3): 286–306.

Baker, T., Connaughton, D., Zhang, J. and Spengler, O. (2007) 'Perceived Risk of Terrorism and Related Risk Management Practices of NCAA Division 1A Football Stadium Managers', *Journal of Legal Aspects of Sport* 17(1): 27–51.

Bakir, V. (2010) 'Media and Risk: Old and New Research Directions', *Journal of Risk Research* 13(1): 5–18.

BBC (2018) 'Premier League TV Rights: Five of Seven Live Packages Sold for £4.464bn', available from: https://www.bbc.co.uk/sport/football/43002985.

BBC (2020) 'Manchester City v Arsenal Postponed over Coronavirus Fears', available from: https://www.bbc.co.uk/sport/football/51829511#:~:text=Manchester%20City's%20Premier%20League%20match, owner%20Evangelos%20Marinakis%20contracted%20coronavirus.

Beck, U. (1992) *Risk Society: Towards a New Modernity*, London: Sage.

Boyle, P. and Haggerty, K.D. (2012) 'Planning for the Worst: Risk, Uncertainty and the Olympic Games', *The British Journal of Sociology* 63(2): 241–259.

Clarkson, B.G., Culvin, A., Pope, S. and Parry, K. (2022) 'Covid-19: Reflections on Threat and Uncertainty for the Future of Elite Women's Football in England', *Managing Sport and Leisure* 27(1–2): 50–61.

Cleland, J. (2019) 'Sports Fandom in the Risk Society: Analyzing Perceptions and Experiences of Risk, Security and Terrorism at Elite Sports Events', *Sociology of Sport Journal* 36(2): 144–151.

Cleland, J. and Cashmore, E. (2018) 'Nothing Will Be the Same Again after the Stade de France Attack: Reflections of Association Football Fans on Terrorism, Security and Surveillance', *Journal of Sport and Social Issues* 42(6): 454–469.

Cottle, S. (1998) 'Ulrich Beck, Risk Society and the Media: A Catastrophic View?', *European Journal of Communication* 13(1): 5–32.

Crawford, A. and Hutchinson, S. (2016) 'Mapping the Contours of 'Everyday Security': Time, Space and Emotion', *The British Journal of Criminology* 56(6): 1184–1202.

Dryhurst, S. et al. (2020) 'Risk Perceptions of COVID-19 around the World', *Journal of Risk Research* 23(7–8): 994–1006.

Feickert, J., Verma, R., Plaschka, G. and Dev, C.S. (2006) 'Safeguarding Your Customers: The Guest's View of Hotel Security', *Cornell Hospitality Quarterly* 47(3): 224–244.

George, R. and Swart, K. (2012) 'International Tourists' Perceptions of Crime–Risk and Their Future Travel Intentions during the 2010 FIFA World Cup™ in South Africa', *Journal of Sport & Tourism* 17(3): 201–223.

Hassan, D. (2016) 'Surveillance by Proxy: Sport and Security in a Modern Age', *American Behavioral Scientist* 60(9):1043–1056.

James, M. and Pearson, G. (2016) 'Legal Responses to Football Crowd Disorder and Violence in England and Wales', *Legal Responses to Football Hooliganism in Europe* (Eds. A. Tsoukala, G. Pearson and P.T.M. Coeneen), The Hague: Springer, pp. 35–52.

Lee Ludvigsen, J.A. (2022) *Sport Mega-Events, Security and Covid-19: Securing the Football World*, London/New York: Routledge.

Lee Ludvigsen, J.A. and Millward, P. (2020) 'A Security Theater of Dreams: Supporters' Responses to "Safety" and "Security" Following the Old Trafford "Fake Bomb" Evacuation', *Journal of Sport and Social Issues* 44(1): 3–21.

Lisle, D. (2016) *Holidays in the Danger Zone*, Minneapolis: University of Minnesota Press.

Liverpool Echo (2020) 'Neutral Venue Idea That Would Affect Liverpool Labelled "Nonsense" by Police Boss', available from: https://www.liverpoolecho.co.uk/sport/football/football-news/neutral-venue-idea-would-affect-18346391.

Lupton, D. (1999) *Risk*, London: Routledge.

Lupton, D. and Tulloch, J. (2002) '"Risk Is a Part of Your Life": Risk Epistemologies among a Group of Australians', *Sociology* 36(2): 317–334.

Millward, P. (2011) *The Global Football League: Transnational Networks, Social Movements and Sport in the New Media Age*, Basingstoke: Palgrave Macmillan.

Millward, P., Lee Ludvigsen, J.A. and Sly, J. (in press) *Sport and Crime: Towards a Critical Criminology of Sport*, Routledge.

Moore, K. (2021) 'Football Is Not 'A Matter of Life and Death'. It Is Far Less Important Than That. Football and the COVID-19 Pandemic in England', *Soccer & Society* 22(1–2): 43–57.

Morgan, N. and Pritchard, A. (2005) 'Security and Social "Sorting": Traversing the Surveillance–Tourism Dialectic', *Tourist Studies* 5(2): 115–132.

Müller, M., Gogishvili, D., Wolfe, S.D., Gaffney, C., Hug, M. and Leick, A. (2021) 'Peak Event: The Rise, Crisis and Decline of Large Events (June 21, 2021)', available at SSRN: https://ssrn.com/abstract=3873972.

Mythen, G. (2018) 'Thinking with Ulrich Beck: Security, Terrorism and Transformation', *Journal of Risk Research* 21(1): 17–28.

Numerato, D. (2018) *Football Fans, Activism and Social Change*, London: Routledge.

Perić, M., Wise, N., Heydari, R., Keshtidar, M. and Mekinc, J. (2021) 'Getting Back to the Event: Covid-19, Attendance and Perceived Importance of Protective Measures', *Kinesiology* 53(1): 12–19.

Poulton, E. (2005) "English Media Representation of Football-Related Disorder: "Brutal, Short-Hand and Simplifying?", *Sport in Society* 8(1): 27–47.

Reddy, M. (2020) Fans Have Been Leading Lights in Their Communities, Not Louts Waiting to Disrupt Football's Return', *The Independent*, available from: https://www.independent.co.uk/sport/football/premier-league/pl-project-restart-when-fans-behind-closed-doors-a9509581.html.

Sky News (2021) 'COVID: Football Fans Say They'll Keep Going to Matches 'For as Long as We're Allowed' - Despite Virus Advice', available from: https://news.sky.com/story/covid-football-fans-say-theyll-keep-going-to-matches-for-as-long-as-were-allowed-despite-virus-advice-12496983.

Stevens, D. and Vaughan-Williams, N. (2017) *Everyday Security Threats: Perceptions, Experiences and Consequences*, Manchester: Manchester University Press.

Tarlow, P. (2002) *Event Risk Management and Safety*, New York: John Wiley and Sons.

Taylor, T and Toohey, K. (2007) 'Perceptions of Terrorism Threats at the 2004 Olympic Games: Implications for Sport Events', *Journal of Sport & Tourism* 12(2): 99–114.

Taylor, T. and Toohey, K. (2015) 'The Security Agencies' Perspective', *Routledge Handbook of Sport Event Management* (Eds. M. Parent and J.L. Chappelet), New York: Routledge, pp. 373–396.

The Daily Mail (2020) 'Revealed: Premier League Sides "Oppose Project Restart's Proposal to Resume Season at Neutral Venues Due to Stadium Sponsorship Deals" with Fears They "Could Have to Pay Back Millions" If They Cannot Play Home', available from: https://www.dailymail.co.uk/sport/sportsnews/article-8308455/Premier-League-sides-oppose-Project-Restarts-neutral-venues-STADIUM-SPONSORSHIP-deals.html.

The Daily Mirror (2020a) 'Police Consulted over Fears Liverpool Fans Could Mob Streets on Day Reds Win Title', available from: https://www.mirror.co.uk/sport/football/news/police-consulted-over-fears-liverpool-21942523.

The Daily Mirror (2020b) 'Every Premier League Club against Playing in Neutral Venues, Says Chief Executive', available from: https://www.mirror.co.uk/sport/football/news/breaking-every-premier-league-club-22009852.

The Guardian (2020) 'UK Coronavirus: Boris Johnson Announces Strict Lockdown across Country – As It Happened', available from: https://www.theguardian.com/politics/live/2020/mar/23/uk-coronavirus-live-news-latest-boris-johnson-minister-condemns-people-ignoring-two-metre-distance-rule-in-parks-as-very-selfish.

The Independent (2016) 'Euro 2016: French Riot Police Fire Tear Gas at Supporters as Fans Told Not to Travel to Eiffel Tower and Champs Elysees', available from: https://www.independent.co.uk/sport/football/international/euro-2016-french-riot-police-fire-tear-gas-at-supporters-outside-paris-fan-zone-during-france-match-against-portugal-a7129906.html.

The Independent (2020) 'Language of Fear around Fans Needs to Be Lost If Premier League Is to Mirror Bundesliga's Successful Return', available from: https://www.independent.co.uk/sport/football/premier-league/project-restart-bundesliga-coronavirus-fan-problems-a9519886.html.

The Telegraph (2020) 'Football's Return? Police Want Season Called Off Altogether If Fans Gather to Watch Games', available from: https://www.telegraph.co.uk/football/2020/04/29/police-will-call-football-season-fans-try-gather-watch-games/?utm_content=telegraph&utm_medium=Social&utm_campaign=Echobox&utm_source=Twitter#Echobox=1588183481.

The Times (2020) 'West Midlands Police and Crime Commissioner David Jamieson Attacks Restart Plans', available from: https://www.thetimes.co.uk/article/west-midlands-police-and-crime-commissioner-david-jamieson-attacks-restart-plans-hl2zkpkts.

Toohey, K., Taylor, T. and Lee, C.K. (2003) 'The FIFA World Cup 2002: The Effects of Terrorism on Sport Tourists', *Journal of Sport Tourism* 8(3): 186–196.

Tsoukala, A. (2008) 'Boundary-Creating Processes and the Social Construction of Threat', *Alternatives* 33(2): 137–152.

Urry, J. and Larsen, J. (2011) *The Tourist Gaze 3.0*, London: Sage.

Webber, D.M. (2021) 'Feasting in a Time of Famine: The English Premier League, "Conspicuous Consumption" and the Politics of Austerity', *Journal of Consumer Culture* 21(3): 598–617.

Wong, D. and Chadwick, S. (2017) 'Risk and (In)Security of FIFA Football World Cups–Outlook for Russia 2018', *Sport in Society* 20(5–6): 583–598.

Zedner, L. (2009) *Security*, London/New York: Routledge.

6 Conclusions and Directions

This final chapter will provide the book's conclusions and directions for both current and future research. Whilst I will argue that football's ability to both reflect and accentuate global risk politics and management is dynamic and perpetual, the book's main conclusions concerning global risks in football must, however, be viewed through an externally positioned socio-political lens that is accurately captured by European football's governing body, Union of European Football Associations (UEFA), that acknowledged that in the current time:

> Risks and incidents in European football continue to be a cause for concern. Conflicts around Europe and the world mean that our continent is more prone than ever to threats. Because football mirrors society, these problems are reflected in football.
>
> (UEFA, n.d.)

The quote above will come with little or no surprise to scholars of sport, who would generally agree that 'sport does not operate in a social vacuum' because, in fact, sport 'is both a product of and a reflection of its social context' (Doidge, 2015: 14). The *sport-mirrors-society* proposition has naturally been illustrated by key developments attributed to globalization, commodification, securitization, mediatization (Lee Ludvigsen, 2022; Numerato and Giulianotti, 2018) and, most recently, by the Covid-19 pandemic and the subsequent 'post-Covid-19 moment' (Lawrence and Crawford, 2022) whose (side-)effects have been mirrored by the worlds of sport and particularly football. As a result, all this means – simply put – that '[t]here can be little doubt football is worthy of serious sociological analysis' (David and Millward, 2012: 351). The motivation behind the idea of utilizing football as a vehicle to understand wider social, cultural and political trends should be positioned beside another influential contestation: namely, that we

DOI: 10.4324/9781003303480–6

presently live in a globalized 'risk society' that is distinctively marked by individuals', institutions' and societies' intensified consciousness of the diverse risks that are 'out there' (Beck, 1992, 1999; Giddens, 1990, 1999).

The two influential and overarching starting points here, relating, first, to utilizing sport's reflections of wider societal developments and, second, to the sociological conceptions of risk's societal dominance, have too rarely been synthesized or cross-fertilized in existing work. Risk theory and scholarly work on football's globalization in football have, too sporadically, been in in-depth conversations. Against such a canvas, this book was primarily set up around two principal aims. First, to explore exactly how football constitutes a crucial and illuminating site for the social sciences' understanding and theorizations of risk that were erected as a scaffold for the remainder of the book in Chapter 2. Second, this book has intended to (re-)energize the field of risk analyses in football (and sport more broadly) by accepting and building largely on Giulianotti's (2009) invitation to sports sociologists to enter the field of risk analysis. The book also tied into an important contention of Cleland (2019) holding that the risk society appears in the minds of many fans who display greater awareness and consciousness of risks related to live sport attendance, whilst it engages with the assertion that:

> Just as other aspects of social life (job market, politics, or environmental protection), *football has also entered the phase of 'second' modernity shaped by global risks*, individualization and cosmopolitanization.
>
> (Kossakowski, 2014: 46, emphasis added)

It is precisely this recognition of the current global phase of football as one shaped by risk that makes it so crucial to bring closer together the two key topics, and meaningfully discuss the ramifications of this.

Hence, this book argues – based on the examples and cases provided across the earlier chapters – that football visibly reflects and has accentuated the broader processes and mechanisms through which risk awareness, aversion, politics and management have intensified and become increasingly global. In part, elite football's position as a quintessential reflector of these risk-related trends emerges from the global flows of people, knowledge, information, capital and consumption practices within it (Chapter 2). Indeed, if it remains 'vital for sociologists to locate risk in sport within [the] contemporary global context' (Giulianotti, 2009: 553), then this book's reconsideration of football has done exactly that, in a timely manner. To this end, the book showcases that football, which is popularly referred to as the 'global game' (Cleland, 2015; Goldblatt, 2019), should be continually employed as a gateway for the reading of the enhanced risk consciousness, management and the transnational scope of unpredictable risks in the contemporary world. This, much in a similar manner to the ways through which sociologists to date – in constructive fashion – have employed football to understand several facets of 'globalization' (e.g., Cleland, 2015; Giulianotti and Robertson, 2009; Millward, 2011), as in a globalized world, risks have essentially taken a 'global turn'. My underlining point is that this is manifested in and accentuated by elite football in the twenty-first century.

These arguments have been developed over this book's separate chapters that unitedly expedite an intellectual journey toward a heightened understanding of risk in football. In this journey, Chapter 1 opened up by setting out the book's key aims and rationales. Chapter 2 built on this and discussed the relationship between 'globalization' and 'risk' whilst laying out the sociological theories and analytical relations for the social study of risk. Then, the remaining chapters have explored environmental and political risks (Chapter 3), the relationship between 'pre-crime' modes of crime control, risk and football (Chapter 4), football fans' perceptions and the media's communications of risk (Chapter 5). To reiterate, I make no claim that the risks discussed throughout this book compose an exhaustive list, a complete atlas or register of the many risks present in football contexts in every corner of the world. But still, those risks discussed throughout the individual chapters best illustrate this book's key points and collectively showcase the constructive, sociologically important but hitherto under-examined position of the 'global game' at the frontiers of our social scientific understanding of 'global risks'.

Notwithstanding, the question of why such an argument *matters* sociologically can now be readdressed. Whilst football's ability to reflect and accelerate wider social or political trends, as discussed above, clearly provides *one* answer to such a question, so does the sport's number of players and spectators, enormous amounts of financial capital and constant presence in the mass media, which all underscore its social significance (Dunning, 1967). Undoubtedly, sport and football in specific are central pillars of modern public life (Giulianotti and Robertson, 2009). Football, in itself, remains 'the most global and most popular of popular cultural phenomenon in the twenty-first century' (Goldblatt, 2019: 3). Yet importantly, this book's arguments are not merely sociologically significant *because football matters*. To recap, the risks, trends and issues discussed throughout here encompass environmental changes and policies, protest and anti-neoliberal globalization activism, political violence, infectious diseases, crime, violence and the media's communication of risks. One commonality here is that all these transcend 'football-specific' contexts and spaces which they have penetrated. Thus, sociologically, they are characterized by a special magnitude as *the* central risks of the twenty-first century. Undoubtedly, the global risks discussed here co-exist, proceed and matter *beyond football*. This again remains important because that means this book illuminates the more general risks which societies, communities, institutions and individuals are faced with, and seek to manage in the present-day, not as confined solely to the domain of football.

This is one of, if not the first, sociological book that focuses specifically on risks in football, and, specifically, it can be claimed that this book makes four key contributions to wider social scientific debates and the sociology of sport, whilst extending the emerging criminology of sport. First, and concerning the former, this work consciously extends, takes forward and updates the palette of risk-related sociological theories (Chapter 2) into a terrain where they too seldom have been meaningfully applied, namely that of contemporary football. Thus, with risk representing a prominent key concept in the social sciences, this book unpacks and advances modern understandings of risk via a football-centred, critical and contemporary investigation: it develops the risk field further through analyses of 'global risk conflict and its particular manifestations through sport events' (Giulianotti, 2009: 552) and football cultures.

Second, this book ties strongly into the existing studies focused on the sport/globalization relationship. Through a discussion of what essentially constitutes the globalization of risks, this work has particularly extended our understanding of what Giulianotti and Robertson (2009: xv) call the 'millennial phase' – which accordingly commenced in 2001 – and is 'distinguished in part by climates of fear alongside the intensification of surveillance and security in social settings'. Though, as the authors admit, this phase was still very much in its preliminary stages in 2009. Thus, this book captures and updates this specific fear-fuelled phase as it has continued apace throughout the 2010s and early 2020s, as a turbulent period characterized by the global effects of, *inter alia*, financial and socio-economic crises, terrorist attacks, (international) political instability, waves of transnational social movements and protests and, most recently, the coronavirus pandemic. Indeed, building upon Giulianotti and Robertson's model, it could be tentatively proposed that the latter composes a phase by itself:

football's *pandemic phase* (late 2019 onwards). Overall, this book connects with and adds to pre-existing academic debates on the impacts of globalization on football (Cleland, 2015; Doidge, 2015; Giulianotti and Robertson, 2007, 2009; Goldblatt, 2019; Millward, 2011).

Third, this work's analysis is also underpinned by, and extends, the growing scholarship on the *nexus* between sport, crime and crime control, which recognizes that sport is a field that, over the last decades, has been penetrated by broader risk logics and social control mechanisms (Groombridge, 2017; Millward et al., in press). Within the developing critical criminology of sport project, this book's discussions of risk logics, crime control (Chapter 4), environmental harms and issues (Chapter 3) and media representations of 'double risks' (Chapter 5) can be considered an extension to the emerging debates on harms and crime control across the critical criminology of sport. The wider importance of this relates to how it reaffirms that criminological perspectives have much to offer the academic study of sport and, more specifically, elite football. Finally, it can be argued that this book makes a telling scholarly contribution through the directions and agendas which it provides for both current and future research, and with its discussions of diverse under-researched case studies such as the EPL's Covid-related 'Project Restart' (Chapter 5) and the World Cup's expansion and upcoming 2026 version (Chapter 3). Therefore, it is hoped that this book's directions, in distinct ways, can work as a social scientific compass that also ignites future inter-disciplinary projects on the relationship between football and risk over the next years.

***

What, or where to next, for the 'global game'? In their concluding reflections on 'global football's future' in 2009, Giulianotti and Robertson (2009: 170) acknowledged that:

> [T]he 'world game' of football will experience a range of internal and external pressures in future years. Many of these pressures will crystallize the increasingly prominent themes of globalization through the twenty-first century.

Up next, where I highlight some current and future lines of research at the beginning of the 2020s, it seems prudent to return to or even echo Giulianotti and Robertson's prediction. Whilst there are several aspects of global football that warrant academic engagement and further sociological imagination, I focus here mostly on four specific yet pressing and transversal themes that can be understood in relation to football's continual global and commercial expansion and external and internal risks. As brought about by both internal and external pressures, these relate to the Covid-19 pandemic, the recent bi-annual World Cup proposal, the 2021 European Super League (ESL) 'breakaway' and decision-aid technologies.

Upon delineating specific research directions, it remains – at the time of writing – difficult to shy away from Covid-19 and its social ramifications. From a risk perspective, Covid-19 represents a new 'world risk' (Beck, 1999) and 'it will take extensive efforts to completely understand and unravel its impacts' (Wardman and Lofstedt, 2020: 834). First, in relation to Covid-19, it is clear that this catastrophe has changed the consumption (Lawrence and Crawford, 2022) and organization (Lee Ludvigsen, 2022) of football in a myriad of ways. In their attempts to minimize the risk of Covid-19 transmission, several football clubs and football authorities have published Covid-specific 'codes of conduct' for match-going supporters returning to stadiums following months with matches behind closed doors or restricted crowds in the 2020/2021 season.[1] Interesting points for future research here relate not merely to how supporters across various (football) cultures and national contexts perceive the risk of Covid-19 upon match attendance, but how the public health risk of Covid-19 is communicated and framed in discourses found in 'code of conducts' or other relevant policy documents or public statements. In reference to Foucauldian perspectives (Chapter 2) and the governance of football spaces and fans, this can ultimately add new layers to our understanding of how discourses and '[f]orms of responsibilisation are nurtured through the diffusion of norms and authorised practices among supporters in regard to "self-policing" and "ambassadorial" conduct' (Giulianotti, 2011: 3303). Such examinations, however, would not merely be an intellectual exercise. Ultimately, empirical findings speaking to how supporters perceive and comply with Covid-19 specific policies may also have practical implications if they can assist the future work of safety officers, stadium managers and other stakeholder groups.

Second, Chapter 3 discussed the expansion of the World Cup concerning the 48-team model and three host countries for 2026. As mentioned, in 2021 reports emerged concerning the possibility of the World Cup being staged bi-annually rather than in the current four-year cycle. In May 2021, FIFA confirmed that a study would be conducted into the feasibility of this proposal. Then, in September 2021, it was reported by FIFA (2021) that this feasibility study – involving a research survey with 23,000 people in 23 countries – demonstrated that: 'The majority of fans would like to see a more frequent men's FIFA World Cup', and that 'Of this majority, the preferred frequency is biennial'.

Upon writing this, it remains unknown whether the World Cup will be staged every two years. Notwithstanding, this would accelerate and revolutionize the cycle of football mega-events and hugely impact the sporting calendar. Critically, this or similar proposals could also increase the demands for host countries willing to stage the largest football spectacle in the world, which already comes at enormous financial and environmental costs (Chapter 3). More frequent World Cups could also likely mean new World Cup-induced stadium constructions or upgrades and increase tournament-related travelling and impacts on social and natural environments. *Prima facie*, the proposal appears highly incompatible with the World Cup's greening initiatives and legacies discussed earlier.

The bi-annual World Cup proposal has, so far, been met by huge scepticism and criticism from fan networks, the World Leagues Forum (Sky Sports, 2021) and UEFA, who threatened to boycott the tournament should it become a reality (The Times, 2021). Meanwhile, the Spanish *La Liga* President, Javier Tebas, framed the idea as a 'threat not just to domestic football leagues but to the overall tradition of world football' (quoted in ESPN, 2021). The proposal to stage the World Cup bi-annually – much like the ESL discussed below – provides an interesting avenue for research on the reputational risks associated with the World Cup itself and FIFA. For instance, researchers could explore fans' perceptions of this proposal and juxtapose this with the mentioned feasibility study that claimed that a 'majority of fans' favoured World Cups more frequently. Further, Kossakowski (2014) reminds us that the self-protection of financial interests may lead to tension and risks between the different organizations and authorities within football. Thus, this serves as an interesting case study for investigations on the relationships between powerful governing bodies and federations in football, as a potential bi-annual World Cup is likely to impact the global popularity of continental mega-events like the European Championships and the Copa America and these tournaments' attractiveness in terms of broadcasting and sponsorship.

Third, in terms of reputational risks and damage and financial risks, it also serves as extremely interesting to explore how the ESL may have caused damages or backlashes for the football clubs associated with the (for now) unsuccessful 2021 ESL 'breakaway'. Indeed, since 1998, European top clubs have toyed with the idea of leaving the UEFA Champions League to set up their own ESL (Van Der Burg, 2021). For the relevant clubs, a membership in the ESL would have provided substantial financial security by removing 'the entrepreneurial risk due to the possibility of not qualifying for the UEFA Champions League' (Brannagan et al., 2022: 171). So, after a period where many clubs had suffered financially due to Covid-19's ripple effects, it was reported on 18 April 2021 that 12 European top clubs from Spain, England and Italy had launched the ESL which would rival the UEFA Champions League (Wagner et al., 2021). However, the 'breakaway' merely lasted approximately 72 hours before nine of the involved clubs announced their withdrawal from the ESL following enormous opposition from athletes, managers, politicians and, crucially, the fans. UEFA threatened the 'breakaway' clubs with sanctions (ibid.), and in some cases, like Manchester United and Chelsea, the clubs' intention to join the ESL caused larger protests by fans gathering outside their respective stadiums on match days. Another backlash following the 'rise and fall' of the ESL was the drop in shares in some of the involved clubs like Juventus and Manchester United (Markets Insider, 2021). Altogether, the ESL proposal serves as an important case for analyzing the reputational risks and its management *vis-à-vis* clubs, owners and sponsors. Such research could, for example, build on Wagner et al.'s (2021) suggestion that the commercial shareholders and club owners misjudged the counter-effects of their press releases in which the ESL break-away was publicly announced.

Lastly, the controversial introduction of the Video Assistant Referee (VAR) decision-aid technology in several top leagues and competitions requires further examination in the coming years. As Chen and Davidson (2021: 44) put it: 'Technology has played a prominent role in not only our daily life but also recently on the soccer pitch'. Yet one may ask how (or if) this relates to risk. To answer that, one rationale behind VAR, as a decision-aid technology, was to minimize and prevent the *risk* of refereeing errors that change the outcome of fixtures. Even though VAR was implemented to make the game less contentious, the system's debut on the global stage in the 2018 World Cup was characterized by enormous controversy and negative media coverage surrounding its performance. Interestingly, the VAR technology, in a way, serves as a symbol of football's techno-scientific advancement. Though, VAR's array of (un)anticipated consequences, its (alleged) objectivity and the scientific approach to referee decision-making can be explored in relation to reflexivity in football and, moreover, be understood as a football-specific and technocratic expert system that is inherently contested and based on heterogeneous interpretations of the same incident or situation which may be considered the 'dialectic of expertise' (Beck, 1992: 30).

Essentially, a critical engagement with the above themes and associated empirical endeavours would not merely help researchers making sense of social life and transformations across football or sport, but the world in which we live wherein 'risk', above all else, is a permanent, prominent and powerful feature that is constantly managed and assigned diverse meanings. Above all, this book, which offers a contemporary update of, and a new context for considering social scientific risk perspectives, demonstrates exactly that.

Note

1 For example, see: https://www.premierleague.com/news/1924451 (Accessed 11/2021).

References

Beck, U. (1992) *Risk Society: Towards a New Modernity*, London: Sage.

Beck, U. (1999) *World Risk Society*, Cambridge: Polity Press.

Brannagan, P., Scelles, N., Valenti, M., Inoue, Y., Grix J. and Perkin, J. (2022) 'The 2021 European Super League Attempt: Motivation, Outcome, and the Future of Football', *International Journal of Sport Policy and Politics* 14(1): 169–176.

Chen, R. and Davidson, N.P. (2022) 'English Premier League Manager Perceptions of Video Assistant Referee (VAR) Decisions during the 2019–2020 Season', *Soccer & Society* 23(1): 44–55.

Cleland, J. (2015) *A Sociology of Football in a Global Context*, London: Routledge.

Cleland, J. (2019) 'Sports Fandom in the Risk Society: Analyzing Perceptions and Experiences of Risk, Security and Terrorism at Elite Sports Events', *Sociology of Sport Journal* 36(2): 144–151.

David, M. and Millward, P. (2012) 'Football's Coming Home?: Digital Reterritorialization, Contradictions in the Transnational Coverage of Sport and the Sociology of Alternative Football Broadcasts', *The British Journal of Sociology* 63(2): 349–369.

Doidge, M. (2015) *Football Italia: Italian Football in an Age of Globalization*, London: Bloomsbury.

Dunning, E. (1967) 'Notes on Some Conceptual and Theoretical Problems in the Sociology of Sport', *International Review of Sport Sociology* 2(1): 143–153.

ESPN (2021) 'UEFA Chief Ceferin Threatens World Cup Boycott If New Plans Go Ahead', available from: https://www.espn.co.uk/football/fifa-world-cup/story/4471415/world-cup-every-two-years-european-club-body-firmly-opposes [Accessed 11/2021].

FIFA (2021) 'Majority of Fans Favour More Frequent Men's FIFA World Cups – Global Survey', available from: https://www.fifa.com/football-development/

the-future-of-football/media-releases/majority-fans-favour-more-frequent-mens-fifa-world-cups-global-survey [Accessed 11/2021].

Giddens, A. (1990) *The Consequences of Modernity*, Cambridge: Polity Press.

Giddens, A. (1999) 'Risk and Responsibility', *The Modern Law Review* 62(1): 1–35.

Giulianotti, R. (2009) 'Risk and Sport: An Analysis of Sociological Theories and Research Agendas', *Sociology of Sport Journal* 26(4): 540–556.

Giulianotti, R. (2011) 'Sport Mega Events, Urban Football Carnivals and Securitised Commodification: The Case of the English Premier League', *Urban Studies* 48(15): 3293–3310.

Giulianotti, R. and Robertson, R. (2007) 'Recovering the Social: Globalization, Football and Transnationalism', *Global Networks* 7(2): 166–186.

Giulianotti, R. and Robertson, R. (2009) *Globalization and Football*, London: Sage.

Goldblatt, D. (2019) *The Age of Football: The Global Game in the Twenty-First Century*, London: Macmillan.

Groombridge, N. (2017) *Sports Criminology: A Critical Criminology of Sport and Games*, Bristol: Policy.

Kossakowski, R. (2014) 'The Cosmopolitan Game? Contemporary Football in the Light of Ulrich Beck's Theory', *Kultura I Edukacja* 5(105): 36–62.

Lawrence, S. and Crawford, G. (2022) 'Towards a Digital Football Studies: Current Trends and Future Directions for Football Cultures Research in the Post-Covid-19 Moment', *Leisure Studies* 41(1): 56–69.

Lee Ludvigsen, J.A. (2022) *Sport Mega-Events, Security and Covid-19: Securing the Football World*, London/New York: Routledge.

Markets Insider (2021) 'Juventus Shares Tumble 14% While Manchester United Slips as European Super League Soccer Plan Implodes', available from: https://markets.businessinsider.com/news/stocks/juventus-manchester-united-stock-price-european-super-league-soccer-2021-4.

Millward, P. (2011) *The Global Football League: Transnational Networks, Social Movements and Sport in the New Media Age*, Basingstoke: Palgrave.

Millward, P., Lee Ludvigsen, J.A. and Sly, J. (in press) *Sport and Crime: Towards a Critical Criminology of Sport*, Routledge.

Numerato, D. and Giulianotti, R. (2018) 'Citizen, Consumer, Citimer: The Interplay of Market and Political Identities within Contemporary Football Fan Cultures', *Journal of Consumer Culture* 18(2): 336–355.

Sky Sports (2021) 'World Cup: FIFA Set to Reveal More Details on Holding Tournament Every Two years', available from: https://www.skysports.com/football/news/11095/12401829/world-cup-fifa-set-to-reveal-more-details-on-holding-tournament-every-two-years [Accessed 11/2021].

The Times (2021) 'UEFA President Aleksander Ceferin: Europe and South America Prepared to Boycott Biennial World Cup', available from: https://www.thetimes.co.uk/article/uefa-president-aleksander-ceferin-europe-and-south-america-prepared-to-boycott-biennial-world-cup-bj3jzmzgh [Accessed 11/2021].

UEFA (n.d.) 'Security', available from: https://www.uefa.com/insideuefa/-protecting-the-game/security/ [Accessed 11/2021].

Van Der Burg, T. (2021) 'A European Super League Would Violate EU Competition Law – As Would UEFA's Proposed Reforms of the Champions League. LSE European Politics and Policy (EUROPP) Blog (20 Feb 2021)', available from: https://blogs.lse.ac.uk/europpblog/2021/02/20/a-european-super-league-would-violate-eu-competition-law-as-would-uefas-proposed-reforms-of-the-champions-league/.

Wagner, U., Storm, R.K. and Cortsen, K. (2021) 'Commercialization, Governance Problems, and the Future of European Football – Or Why the European Super League Is Not a Solution to the Challenges Facing Football', *International Journal of Sport Communication*, 14(3): 321–333.

Wardman, J.K. and Lofstedt, R. (2020) 'COVID-19: Confronting a New World Risk', *Journal of Risk Research* 23(7–8): 833–837.

Index

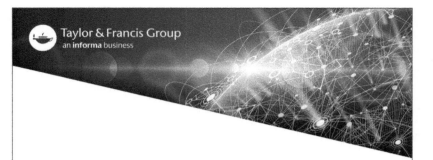

www.ingramcontent.com/pod-product-compliance
Ingram Content Group UK Ltd.
Pitfield, Milton Keynes, MK11 3LW, UK
UKHW020425010325
455677UK00029B/1005

9 781032 301136